This book belongs to:

_____

LEISURE ARTS, INC.
Little Rock, Arkansas

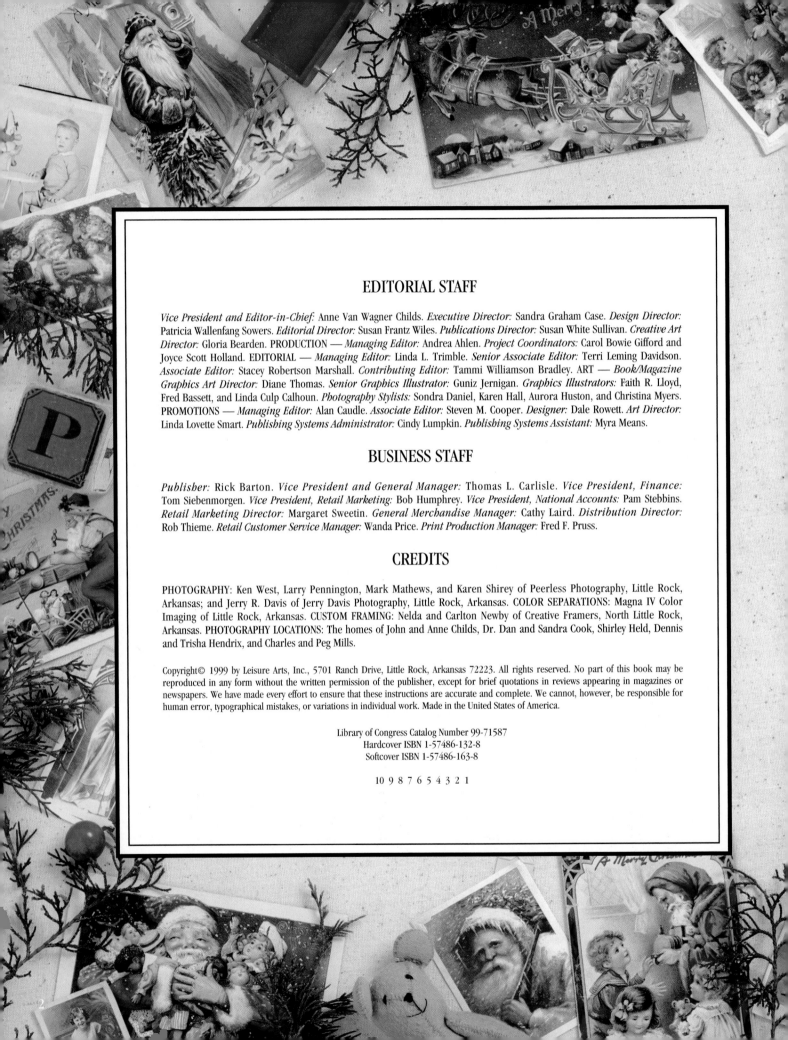

EDITORIAL STAFF

Vice President and Editor-in-Chief: Anne Van Wagner Childs. *Executive Director:* Sandra Graham Case. *Design Director:* Patricia Wallenfang Sowers. *Editorial Director:* Susan Frantz Wiles. *Publications Director:* Susan White Sullivan. *Creative Art Director:* Gloria Bearden. PRODUCTION — *Managing Editor:* Andrea Ahlen. *Project Coordinators:* Carol Bowie Gifford and Joyce Scott Holland. EDITORIAL — *Managing Editor:* Linda L. Trimble. *Senior Associate Editor:* Terri Leming Davidson. *Associate Editor:* Stacey Robertson Marshall. *Contributing Editor:* Tammi Williamson Bradley. ART — *Book/Magazine Graphics Art Director:* Diane Thomas. *Senior Graphics Illustrator:* Guniz Jernigan. *Graphics Illustrators:* Faith R. Lloyd, Fred Bassett, and Linda Culp Calhoun. *Photography Stylists:* Sondra Daniel, Karen Hall, Aurora Huston, and Christina Myers. PROMOTIONS — *Managing Editor:* Alan Caudle. *Associate Editor:* Steven M. Cooper. *Designer:* Dale Rowett. *Art Director:* Linda Lovette Smart. *Publishing Systems Administrator:* Cindy Lumpkin. *Publishing Systems Assistant:* Myra Means.

BUSINESS STAFF

Publisher: Rick Barton. *Vice President and General Manager:* Thomas L. Carlisle. *Vice President, Finance:* Tom Siebenmorgen. *Vice President, Retail Marketing:* Bob Humphrey. *Vice President, National Accounts:* Pam Stebbins. *Retail Marketing Director:* Margaret Sweetin. *General Merchandise Manager:* Cathy Laird. *Distribution Director:* Rob Thieme. *Retail Customer Service Manager:* Wanda Price. *Print Production Manager:* Fred F. Pruss.

CREDITS

PHOTOGRAPHY: Ken West, Larry Pennington, Mark Mathews, and Karen Shirey of Peerless Photography, Little Rock, Arkansas; and Jerry R. Davis of Jerry Davis Photography, Little Rock, Arkansas. COLOR SEPARATIONS: Magna IV Color Imaging of Little Rock, Arkansas. CUSTOM FRAMING: Nelda and Carlton Newby of Creative Framers, North Little Rock, Arkansas. PHOTOGRAPHY LOCATIONS: The homes of John and Anne Childs, Dr. Dan and Sandra Cook, Shirley Held, Dennis and Trisha Hendrix, and Charles and Peg Mills.

Library of Congress Catalog Number 99-71587
Hardcover ISBN 1-57486-132-8
Softcover ISBN 1-57486-163-8

10 9 8 7 6 5 4 3 2 1

INTRODUCTION

From the earliest days of Christianity — and even before — one man has embodied the ideal of kindness and generosity that we've forever held dear. He has many names the world over: St. Nicholas, Weihnachtsmann, Father Christmas, Père Noël, or simply Santa. But he is eternally the renowned ambassador of joy and goodwill. Even now, at the advent of a new millennium, the most famous of gift bearers waits expectantly at his Arctic workshop to renew the childlike wonder in each of us. Santa Claus. The mention of his name evokes the treasured memories of a childhood friend who rejoins us at each Yuletide celebration. Turn the page and step back in time as we trace his rich heritage throughout Europe and onto the shores of the New World. The vintage portraits included in this nostalgic journey were gleaned from antique lithographs and postcards and lovingly adapted into heirloom-quality cross stitch. As you peruse the history and stitch the designs, we hope you'll experience the special joy that the dear elf has carried through the ages.

THE HISTORY OF
santa claus

As we step into the dawn of a new millennium, it's fitting to pause and reflect on the colorful traditions that have spanned history — especially those beloved figures who are as vivid today as in any other era. One such personality is the jolly old elf himself ... Santa Claus.

He hasn't always looked like the crimson-clad fellow we know today. Like so many other traditions in our country, he's a product of the great American melting pot — a blending of many different cultures and customs. His earliest ancestors date back to pre-Christian days, when sky-riding deities were the celebrated gods of earth. The mythological characters Odin, Thor, and Saturn gave us the basis for many of Santa's distinctive characteristics.

But the most influential figure in the shaping of today's generous Santa Claus was a real man, St. Nicholas of Myra (now Turkey), a fourth-century bishop. As a champion of children and the needy, he was legendary for his kindness and generosity.

A TRADITION
OF BENEVOLENCE

In a well-known story illustrating St. Nicholas' benevolence, we find two basic principles of the holiday spirit — giving to others and helping the less fortunate — as well as the tradition of hanging stockings by the fireplace.

According to this legend, there were three Italian maidens whose family had fallen on hard times. Because their father couldn't afford the dowries necessary for them to marry, he was considering selling one of his daughters into slavery in order to provide the dowries for the other two. When the good saint heard of the family's plight, he went to their home late one night and anonymously tossed three bags of gold down the chimney. Miraculously, a bag fell into each of the sisters' stockings, which were hanging by the fire to dry. His kindhearted gift made it possible for all three maidens to happily marry.

A variation of this story is that as each girl was ready to wed, St. Nicholas came in the middle of the night when no one could see him and tossed a bag of gold through an open window into her stocking. This idea of gifts being delivered through an open window may have begun as a way to explain how Santa enters homes that have no chimney.

PATRON SAINT

Because of his wisdom and sensitivity, many groups claimed St. Nicholas as their patron saint. Children, orphans, sailors, and even thieves often prayed to the compassionate saint for guidance and protection. Entire countries, including Russia and Greece, also adopted him as their patron saint, as well as students and pawnbrokers.

Throughout his life, St. Nicholas tried to help others while also inspiring them to imitate his virtues. Legends of his unselfish giving spread all over northern Europe, and accounts of his heroic deeds blended with regional folklore. Eventually, the image of the stately saint was transformed into an almost mystical being, one known for rewarding the good and punishing the bad.

The date of his death, December 6th, was honored with an annual feast, which came to mark the beginning of the medieval Christmas season. On St. Nicholas' Eve, youngsters would set out food for the saint, straw for his horse, and schnapps for his attendant. The next morning, obedient children awoke to find their gifts replaced with sweets and toys, but naughty ones found their offerings untouched alongside a rod or bundle of switches. St. Nicholas' Day is still observed in many countries, and gifts are exchanged in honor of his spirit of brotherhood and charity.

THE MAKING OF SANTA CLAUS

After the Protestant Reformation in the sixteenth century, the feasting and veneration of Catholic saints were banned. But people had become accustomed to the annual visit from their gift-giving saint and didn't want to forget the purpose of the holiday. So in some countries, the festivities of St. Nicholas' Day were merged with Christmas celebrations, and although the gift-bearer took on new, non-religious forms, he still reflected the saint's generous spirit.

In Germany, he appeared as Weihnachtsmann, in England as Father Christmas, and in France as Père Noël, who left small gifts in the children's shoes.

In the areas where St. Nicholas was still portrayed as the gift-bringer, a host of other characters developed as his assistants. Two of his most well-known helpers were Knecht Ruprecht and the Belsnickel. Depending on the local tradition, they were either attendants to St. Nicholas or gift-bearers themselves; but in all cases, both were fearsome characters, brandishing rods or switches. It was their duty not only to reward good children but also to reprove children who were naughty or couldn't recite their prayers.

Knecht Ruprecht (meaning Servant Rupert) was also known by other names such as Black Peter (so called because he delivered the presents down the chimney for St. Nicholas and became blackened with soot).

In some places, the images of Knecht Ruprecht and St. Nicholas merged to form Ru Klaus (meaning Rough Nicholas — so named for his rugged appearance),

Aschen Klaus (or Ash Nicholas — because he carried a sack of ashes and a bundle of switches), and Pelznickel (translated as "Furry Nicholas" — referring to his fur-clad appearance).

When the Germans settled Pennsylvania in the eighteenth century, they brought stories of their Belsnickel. With his Old World custom of meting out rewards and punishments, he frightened even the most well-behaved children, yet his yearly visit was eagerly anticipated. Not all of St. Nicholas' companions were frightening. In fact, the Christkindl (meaning Christ Child) was thought to accompany him in many countries. Often portrayed by a fair-haired young girl, this angelic figure was sometimes the gift-bearer, too. It is believed that the slurred pronunciation of the name Christkindl gave rise to another of Santa's pseudonyms, Kriss Kringle.

SANTA IN AMERICA

Immigrants to the New World brought along their diverse beliefs when they crossed the Atlantic. The Scandinavians introduced gift-giving elves, the Germans brought not only their Belsnickel and Christkindl, but also their decorated trees, and the Irish contributed the ancient Gaelic custom of placing a lighted candle in the window. In the 1600's, the Dutch presented Sinterklaas (meaning St. Nicholas) to the Colonies. In their excitement, many English-speaking children uttered the name so quickly that Sinterklaas sounded like "Sainty Claus." After years of mispronunciation, the name evolved into Santa Claus.

In 1808, American author Washington Irving created a new version of old St. Nick. This one rode over the treetops in a horse-drawn wagon "dropping gifts down the chimneys of his favorites." In his satire, Diedrich Knickerbocker's *History of New York from the Beginning of the World to the End of the Dutch Dynasty*, Irving described Santa as a jolly Dutchman who smoked a long-stemmed clay pipe and wore baggy breeches and a broad-brimmed hat. Also, the familiar phrase, "...laying a finger beside his nose...," first appeared in Irving's story.

That phrase was used again in 1822 in the now-classic poem by Dr. Clement Clarke Moore, "A Visit from St. Nicholas," more commonly known as "The Night Before Christmas." His verse gave an Arctic flavor to Santa's image when he substituted eight tiny reindeer and a sleigh for Irving's horse and wagon. It is Moore's description of Santa that we most often think of today: "He had a broad face, and a little round belly, that shook, when he laughed, like a bowl full of jelly."

Up to this point, Santa's physical appearance and the color of his suit were open to individual interpretation. Then in 1863, Thomas Nast, a German immigrant, gave us a visual image of the cheerful giver that was to later become widely accepted.

When Nast was asked to illustrate Moore's charming verse for a book of children's poems, he gave us a softer, kinder Santa who was still old but appeared less stern than the ecclesiastical St. Nicholas. He dressed his elfin figure in red and endowed him with human characteristics. Most importantly, Nast gave Santa a home at the North Pole. For twenty-three years, his annual Christmas drawings for *Harper's Weekly* magazine allowed Americans to peek into the magical world of Santa Claus and set the stage for the shaping of today's merry gentleman.

Artist Haddon Sundblom added the final touches to Santa's modern image. Beginning in 1931, his billboards and other advertisements for Coca-Cola® featured a portly, grandfatherly Santa with human proportions and a ruddy complexion. Sundblom's exuberant, twinkling-eyed Santa firmly fixed the gift-giver's image in the public mind.

St. Nicholas' evolution into today's happy, larger-than-life Santa Claus is a wonderful example of the blending of countless beliefs and practices from around the world. This benevolent figure encompasses all the goodness and innocence of childhood. And because goodness is his very essence, in every kindness we do, Santa will always be remembered.

TABLE OF CONTENTS

	PHOTO	CHART
Saint Nicholas of Myra	9	52-53
Sinterklaas	11	54-55
Ru Klaus	13	56-57
Santa in Furs	15	58-59
Père Noël	17	60-61
With the Christkindl	19	62-63
Grandfather Frost	21	64-65
Weihnachtsmann	23	66-67
Joulupukki	25	68-69
Father Christmas in Crimson	27	70-71
Jolly Old Elf	29	72-73
Santa's Workshop	31	74-75
St. Nick	33	76-77
Victorian Santa	35	78-79
Yuletide Patriot	37	80-81
Merry Old Santa	39	82-83
A Saintly Tradition	41	84-85
Department Store Santa	43	86-87
Sincerely, Santa	45	88-89
Christmas Patches	47	90-91
Checking His List	49	92-93
Hooray for Christmas	51	94-95
General Instructions		96

SAINT NICHOLAS OF MYRA

The holiday traditions of Santa,
so familiar to us now, were born in
the legendary generosity of a fourth-
century bishop, Saint Nicholas of Myra.
Ministering in the land now called Turkey,
he is said to have performed many
miracles, the most famous of which was
aiding the daughters of a peasant who
could not afford their dowries. When time
came for the girls to wed, the priest secretly
tossed gold coins down the chimney and
into stockings hung by the fireside to dry.
The small gifts made it possible for the
maidens to marry, saving them from
a destiny of slavery. As such legends
spread across Europe, the revered saint
was honored with a feast day on
December 6 — St. Nicholas's Day.

SINTERKLAAS

*T*he image of St. Nicholas has evolved through the ages from the ecclesiastical visage of a bishop into a figure whose attire blends a variety of customs. Each culture imparted a unique characteristic, which helped endear him wherever he traveled. Children in the Low Countries of northern Europe, for example, naturally envisioned their gift-bearer traversing through the snow wearing the traditional wooden clogs of Holland. When the Dutch came to the New World in the early 1600's, they introduced their Sinterklaas to a new land where, to the ears of the colonists, he became "Santa Claus."

Chart on pages 54-55

RU KLAUS

Although Christianity had encompassed Europe before the Middle Ages, many people in these lands continued to incorporate ancient pagan traditions into their Catholic doctrine. One such legend of the Germanic region told of a shaggy, dark man who appeared at the Winter Solstice, the shortest day of the year. He heralded the warmth of the coming season, and his gifts of fruit and nuts held the promise of plentiful crops to come. When the observance of Christ's mass — or Christmas — replaced the mid-winter festival, the gruff figure began to blend with the portrayal of St. Nicholas and came to be known as Ru Klaus or Rauklas (Rough Nicholas).

Chart on pages 56-57

SANTA IN FURS

Another Christmas servant of Old
World Germany was Pelznickel, also
known as Der Belsnickel or "Nicholas
in Furs." Unlike the genteel saint,
Belsnickel was a mischievous character
who enjoyed frightening children by
rattling branches over windowpanes as
he approached, only to soften his mood
and offer sweets at the door. Gradually
"Belsnickeling" became the custom of
going door-to-door collecting food
and money for the needy — a custom
brought to the New World by the
Pennsylvania Deutsch. Over time,
the traditions of the rugged Belsnickel
and the gracious St. Nick merged,
and the blended image continued
to appear into the late 1800's.

Chart on pages 58-59

PÈRE NOËL

Resembling Father Christmas of Britain, Père Noël is the French messenger of Noël, the festival of good news and gifts. His earliest attire was rather meager, but was always accented with evergreens or mistletoe, hearkening the Gallic reverence for nature. Cloaked in the darkness of night, he secretly visited the children on Christmas Eve, leaving tokens in their shoes by the hearth. During the 1700's, his legend migrated into the Louisiana Territory with the colorful Cajun settlers, who gave him a twinkling wit and an eye for the ladies.

Chart on pages 60-61

WITH THE CHRISTKINDL

In time, the Protestant reformers in Germany halted the veneration of Catholic saints, including the beloved Saint Nicholas. His role as benevolent gift-bearer was replaced in the southern regions by the Christkindl, or Christ Child, a cherubic depiction of the Baby Jesus. Understandably, the traditions were often combined, with the rugged folk figure Ru Klaus accompanying the ethereal Babe as he traveled by mule or ram distributing gifts. Children welcomed the pair on Christmas Eve by setting out baskets of hay for the steed, waking to find them filled with snits (dried apple slices) and choosets (candy). By the mid-1800's, however, the Christkindl evolved into Kriss Kringle, a figure very similar to our Santa Claus.

Chart on pages 62 -63

19

GRANDFATHER FROST

As the patron saint of Russia, Saint Nicholas was an especially revered presence in the Orthodox Church. Rather than being symbzolic of Christmas, however, the saint enjoyed his own feast day on December 6. The figure Russians more closely associated with Christmas was Dedt Moroz (Father Ice), a wintry character from an ancient folk tale who richly rewarded kindness and harshly punished wickedness. With the rise of communism, Christianity and its traditions were outlawed, so a new folk hero — Grandfather Frost — emerged combining characteristics of Saint Nicholas and Father Ice. Today, he resembles the Western Santa Claus, but only bears gifts for New Year's Day.

Chart on pages 64-65

WEIHNACHTSMANN

*T*he Weihnachtsmann was a secular
version of St. Nicholas who made his
appearance in northern Germany by the
1800's. One of the few Christmas fellows
who was actually seen by children, he
traveled about on Christmas Eve, walking
from place to place with a sack or basket
of gifts. Though usually viewed as a
kindly gift-bearer, he also carried sticks
meant for bad children. In some provinces,
the Weihnachtsmann's visit was preceded
by the Christkindl, who made a list of
children's wishes and then dispatched
the old gent to deliver the presents
late in the afternoon while families
attended church services.

Chart on pages 66-67

23

JOULUPUKKI

From Finland comes the pagan legend of Joulupukki, literally meaning "Yule Buck." This sprightly fellow did not offer gifts, but rather demanded them as payment for warding off evil spirits. Variations of this tradition remained strong in Scandinavian countries, but gradually took on a Christian flavor as the eras passed. Eventually, he assumed the persona of Santa Claus, but remained one of the few gentlemen whom children could actually see in the act of delivering gifts. It is likely that this snowy land, which is close to the North Pole, gave us one lasting Christmas tradition — that of Santa's reindeer.

24

Chart on pages 68-69

FATHER CHRISTMAS IN CRIMSON

Similar to other European legends, Father Christmas was the central figure in the English Yuletide celebration. He was not descended from Saint Nicholas, however, but filtered from the early Roman and Druid influences. Initially, he was more concerned with bringing mistletoe and wassail — the traditional fruity mulled ale of the season — than with delivering presents to mindful children. However, he grew into the role of kindly gift-giver by the late 1700's, before crossing the Atlantic with immigrants to America. It was here that he reunited with legends from around the world and began his transformation into the red-cloaked Santa Claus.

Chart on pages 70-71

JOLLY OLD ELF

One of our earliest peeks at a modern Santa Claus can be found in Washington Irving's satire, "Knickerbocker's History of New York," which was published in 1809 under the pseudonym Diedrich Knickerbocker. The book highlighted many of the old Dutch traditions about Saint Nick, painting him as a sprightly fellow who arrived by horseback and disappeared up the chimney by "laying his finger beside his nose." Many of those images reappeared in 1823 within Clement Clarke Moore's immortal poem, "A Visit from St. Nicholas" — perhaps more widely recognized as "The Night Before Christmas." Adding Arctic flavor, Moore changed the horse to the "eight tiny reindeer" that we know today.

Chart on pages 72-73

SANTA'S WORKSHOP

The conventional vision of Santa Claus in the 1800's did not include a legion of elves — instead Santa himself was widely depicted in elfin proportions. He toiled alone at his North Pole home, building trains and tops and painting personalities on dolls and tin soldiers. In time, the folklore of Scandinavia added another facet to the Yuletide legend — the Nordic tradition of gift-giving elves. These wee workers gradually joined Santa at his frosty retreat, and helped fulfill his growing lists of wishes.

Chart on pages 74-75

ST. NICK

The verses penned by Clement Clarke Moore painted an indelible image in the imaginations of America's children. They adored Santa's broad face, droll mouth, and little round belly that shook under an infectious, booming laugh. He was no longer a gaunt figure or reverent bishop, but a jolly benefactor who was affectionately known as "St. Nick" for short. But to truly see the works of his magic, little ones had to be on their very best behavior. And, oh, how they longed to see their names inscribed in his list of "Good Boys and Girls" — rather than the bad!

Chart on pages 76-77

VICTORIAN SANTA

In the 1850's, a fashionable women's magazine detailed the Yuletide celebration of the British royal family, sparking a new ardor for the holiday observance. Sentimental Victorians — influenced by Prince Albert's German traditions — adopted such emblems as the richly adorned Christmas tree and even contrived new ways to share their gaiety with loved ones. Holiday postcards and greeting cards soon came into vogue, and naturally one of the most popular subjects was Santa Claus, a descendant of Britain's own Father Christmas. These mementos not only conveyed the salutations of the day, but many have been preserved as mementos of that nostalgic era.

Chart on pages 78-79

YULETIDE
PATRIOT

Santa was such a beloved character in American lore that he often was depicted as a flag-waving patriot. When the dark days of the Civil War clouded the Yuletide of 1862, President Lincoln sought to use Santa's good will as a way to uplift his lonesome troops. He asked Harper's Weekly illustrator Thomas Nast — a German immigrant and vigorous opponent of slavery — to draw Santa bringing comfort to a Union regiment. Gleaning ideas from Clement Moore's verses about the elf, Nast combined them with the personified symbol of the country, Uncle Sam. The result was a jolly, round man clad in a suit of stars and stripes. An inspiring creation, it was called "one of the most demoralizing moments for the Confederate army."

Chart on pages 80-81

MERRY OLD SANTA

An appearance of St. Nick in Harper's Weekly during the Civil War was so popular, it became a Christmas tradition for the magazine. Over the next 40 years, the stars and stripes of Santa's wardrobe were shed in favor of a plain wool coat, which then evolved into a vibrant fur-trimmed suit. Thomas Nast added other unique elements each year of his tenure, such as Santa poring over a list of naughty and nice children, crafting toys in his North Pole workshop, or whisking away in his reindeer-drawn sleigh. One of the artist's later contributions, the familiar pipe-smoking fellow shown here, illustrates the indelible nature of Nast's vision. Through the magazine's wide influence, his creations became the accepted rendition of America's own Santa Claus.

A SAINTLY TRADITION

Revived in 19th-Century England, the custom of hanging stockings by the fire evolved from Saint Nicholas' legendary offering to three impoverished maidens. Children have long relished the ceremony of hanging their stockings on the mantel in hopes of finding them filled with toys at dawn. After all, how could Santa emerge from his descent down the chimney without seeing them dangling expectantly! In homes without chimneys, however, Santa often discovers stockings strung along a windowsill, or perhaps shoes strategically placed by the door.

Chart on pages 8

Department Store Santa

As early as the 1830's, merchants had discovered the worth of Christmas shoppers and devised enticements for their patronage. Newspapers were filled with advertisements, hawking such hard-to-acquire treasures as fresh fruit and manufactured toys or books and pianofortes. Although we take it for granted seeing Santa at all the shopping centers today, he actually began to appear on street corners and in department stores before 1850. Store owners in Philadelphia were among the first to offer seasonal employment to Santa stand-ins. A department store even helped build on the holiday legend — Rudolph the Red-Nosed Reindeer was created in 1939 by an advertising writer for the Montgomery Ward Company.

Chart on pages 86-87

SINCERELY, SANTA

Children have found many clever ways to tell Santa of their Christmas wishes. Messages may be tucked into shoes or laid on the hearth, and some children are lucky enough to tell him in person when he comes to their doors. American children often sit on St. Nick's lap at a store and whisper in his ear, or they may jot their desires in a letter bound for the North Pole. Little ones in Britain also write their requests to Father Christmas; but instead of dropping them in the mailbox, the letters are tossed into the fireplace. The draught then carries their sentiments up the chimney, and the jolly gent reads them in the smoke. Yet no matter what the means he learns of their dreams, Santa takes special note and does his best to make them come true.

Chart on pages 88-89

CHRISTMAS PATCHES

Images of Santa continue to evolve, effected by the fashions of the day. He's even been known to adopt the folksy style of contemporary Americana, donning a quaint patchwork ensemble. The long robe hearkens back to his ecclesiastical ancestor, the Bishop of Myra, in an example of how Santa changes, yet remains the same benevolent chap. In prosperous days and in times of need, Santa always finds his way through the night, bringing the love and cheer of Christmas.

Chart on pages 90-91

checking his list

As he readies for his epic voyage, St. Nick pauses for one last review of his fabled list of little ones, ensuring that every good deed is noted and rewarded. He sees our every deed, as reflected in the Yuletide melodies we know by heart. Whether we're pouting or crying, sleeping or awake, he mystically knows if we've been naughty or nice. It's an admonishment that has spurred the best behavior of many an impish child. After all, it's time to mind your manners when Santa Claus is coming to town!

Chart on pages 92 - 93

HOORAY FOR CHRISTMAS

An animated blend of whimsy
and wit, today's Santa is the colorful
product of a thousand-year evolution.
He's nimble and sprightly with a
gleam in his eye, unable to contain his
Christmas Day excitement! To each
toy he creates, Santa imparts a bit
of his magical joy, perhaps because he's
still a bit of a child himself — in
spite of his age. The future may bring
more changes in St. Nick's face or
fashion, but he will forever be
our sentry of unabashed glee.

Chart on pages 94 -95

SAINT NICHOLAS OF MYRA

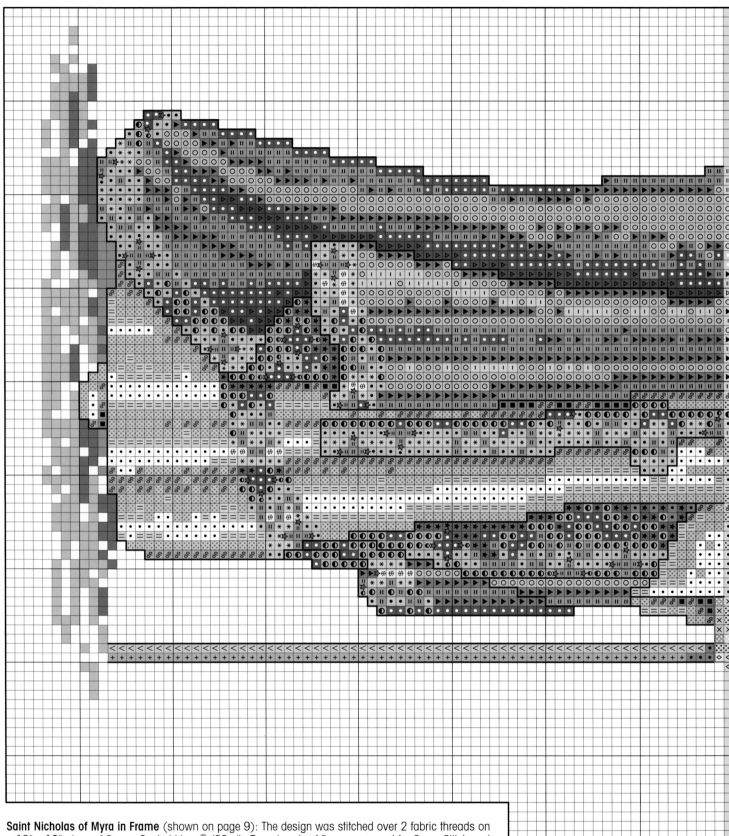

Saint Nicholas of Myra in Frame (shown on page 9): The design was stitched over 2 fabric threads on a 13" x 19" piece of Cream Cashel Linen® (28 ct). Two strands of floss were used for Cross Stitch and 1 strand for Half Cross Stitch and Backstitch. Attach beads using 1 strand of DMC 3721 floss for red beads and 1 strand of DMC 729 floss for gold beads. See Attaching Beads, page 96. It was custom framed.

Needlework adaptation by Carol Emmer.

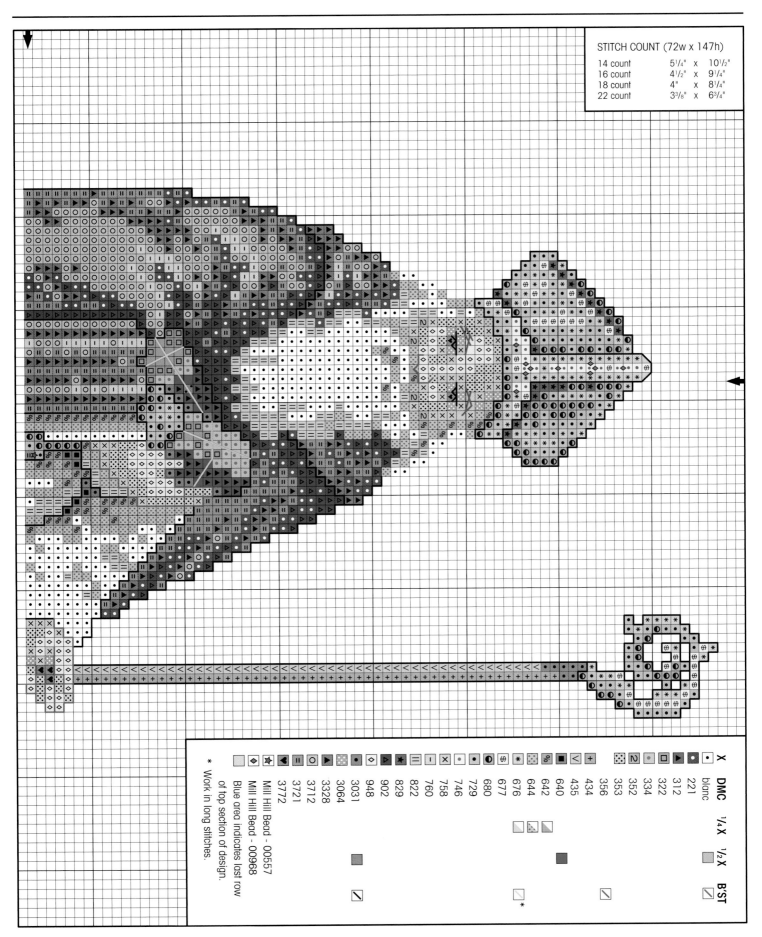

STITCH COUNT (72w x 147h)

14 count	5¼" x	10½"
16 count	4½" x	9¼"
18 count	4" x	8¼"
22 count	3³⁄₈" x	6¾"

DMC	¼X	½X	B'ST
X			
blanc			
221			
312			
322			
334			
352			
353			
356			
434			
435			
640		▨	▨
642			
644		▨	▨ *
676			
677			
680			
729			
746			
758			
760			
822			
829			
902			
948			
3031	▨		▨
3064			
3328			
3712			
3721			
3772			
Mill Hill Bead - 00968			
Mill Hill Bead - 00557			

* Blue area indicates last row
of top section of design.
* Work in long stitches.

53

SINTERKLAAS

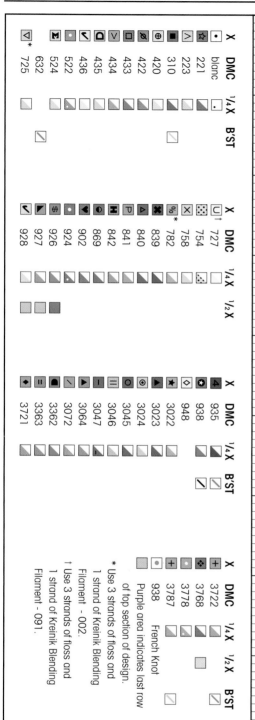

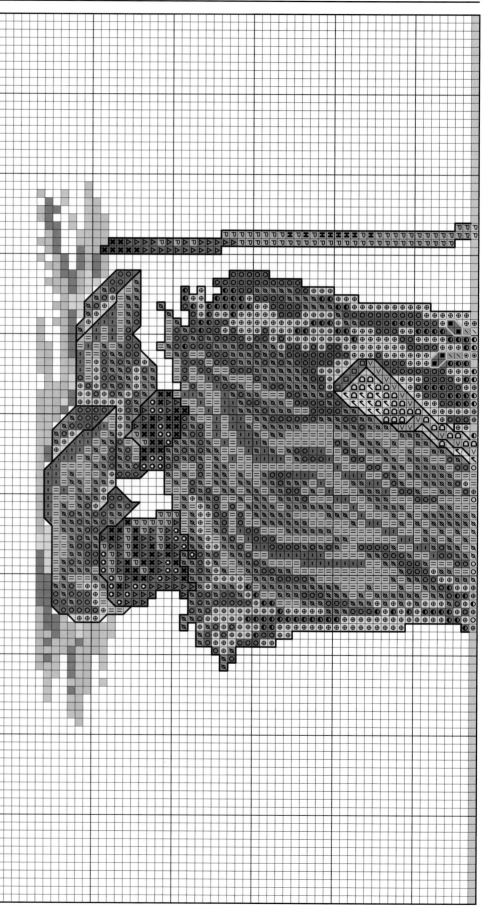

Sinterklaas in Frame (shown on page 11): The design was stitched over 2 fabric threads on a 13" x 18" piece of Amsterdam Blue Cashel Linen® (28 ct). Three strands of floss were used for Cross Stitch and 1 strand for Half Cross Stitch, Backstitch, and French Knots, unless otherwise noted in the color key. It was custom framed.

Needlework adaptation by
Donna Vermillion Giampa.

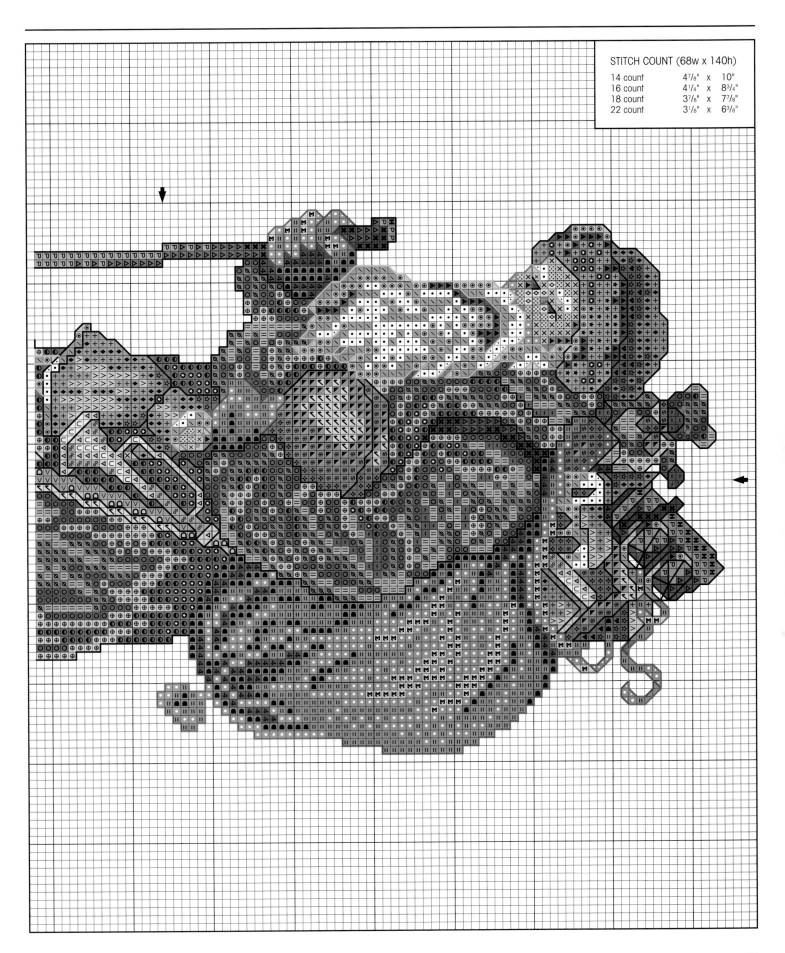

ru klaus

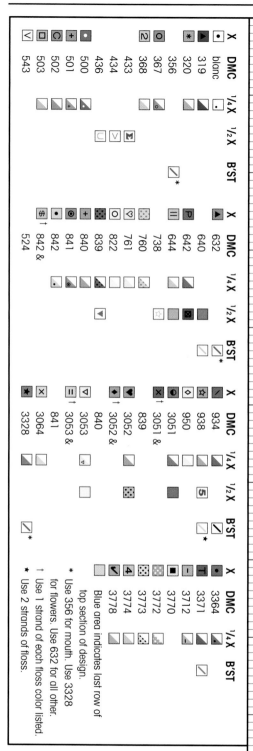

X	¼X	½X	B'ST	DMC
▽	◺			543
▣	◺			503
◠	◺			502
✚	◹			501
▢	◺			500
▨				436
②				434
O				433
●	◺			368
▶	◹			367
▶	◺			356
★	◺			320
✱	◺	C	◺	319
・	・	V M	*	blanc

X	¼X	½X	B'ST	DMC
▶	◺			632
≡	P			640
O	◁	◀	◺	642
+	◺			644
◉	◎			738
◉	●			760
$	◺		*	761
	◺			822
	◺			839
	◺			840
	◺			841
	◺			842
	◺			842 &
	◺			524

X	¼X	½X	B'ST	DMC
★	◺		◺	934
✕	◺		◺	938
		■	*	950
‖	M			3051
▼				3051 &
◆				3052
◀				3052 &
✕	◺			839
◐	◺			3053
◇	◁			3053 &
☆				841
╱	◺	⑤		3064
				3328

X	¼X	½X	B'ST	DMC
▢	◺		◺	3364
◥	◣			3371
④				3712
▨	◺			3770
■	◺			3772
				3773
∣	◺			3774
⊡	⌐			3778

Blue area indicates last row of top section of design.

* Use 356 for mouth. Use 632 for all other. for flowers. Use 356

† Use 1 strand of each floss color listed.

★ Use 2 strands of floss.

Ru Klaus in Frame (shown on page 13): The design was stitched over 2 fabric threads on a 14" x 19" piece of Platinum Cashel Linen® (28 ct). Two strands of floss were used for Cross Stitch and 1 strand for Half Cross Stitch and Backstitch, unless otherwise noted in the color key. It was custom framed.

Needlework adaptation by
Donna Vermillion Giampa.

STITCH COUNT (88w x 153h)

count			
14 count	6³⁄₈"	x	11"
16 count	5¹⁄₂"	x	9⁵⁄₈"
18 count	5"	x	8¹⁄₂"
22 count	4"	x	7"

SANTA IN FURS

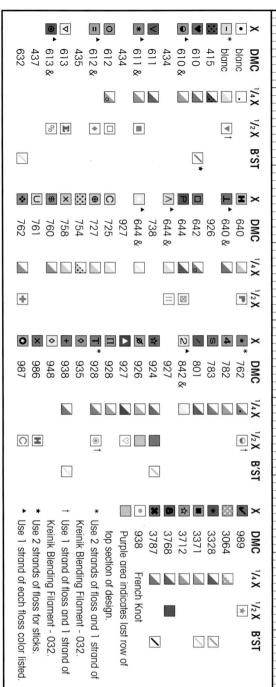

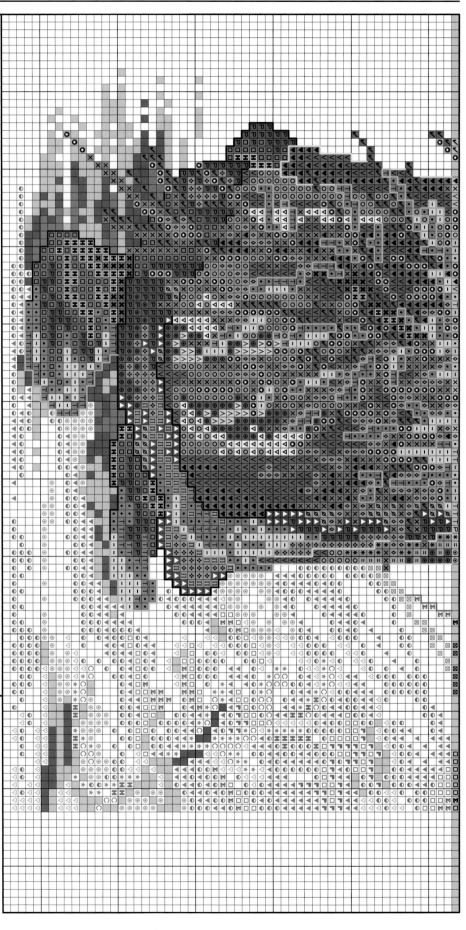

Santa in Furs in Frame (shown on page 15): The design was stitched over 2 fabric threads on a 15" x 19" piece of Confederate Grey Cashel Linen® (28 ct). Two strands of floss were used for Cross Stitch and 1 strand for Half Cross Stitch, Backstitch, and French Knots, unless otherwise noted in the color key. It was custom framed.

Needlework adaptation by Donna Vermillion Giampa.

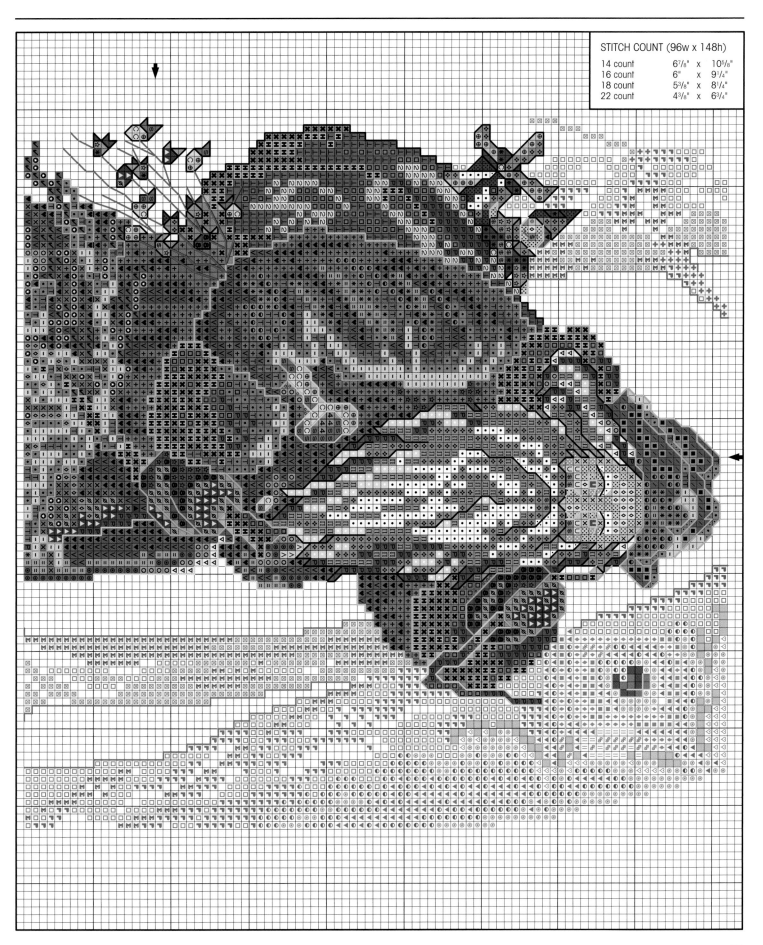

STITCH COUNT (96w x 148h)

14 count	6⁷/₈"	x	10⁵/₈"
16 count	6"	x	9¹/₄"
18 count	5³/₈"	x	8¹/₄"
22 count	4³/₈"	x	6³/₄"

Père Noël

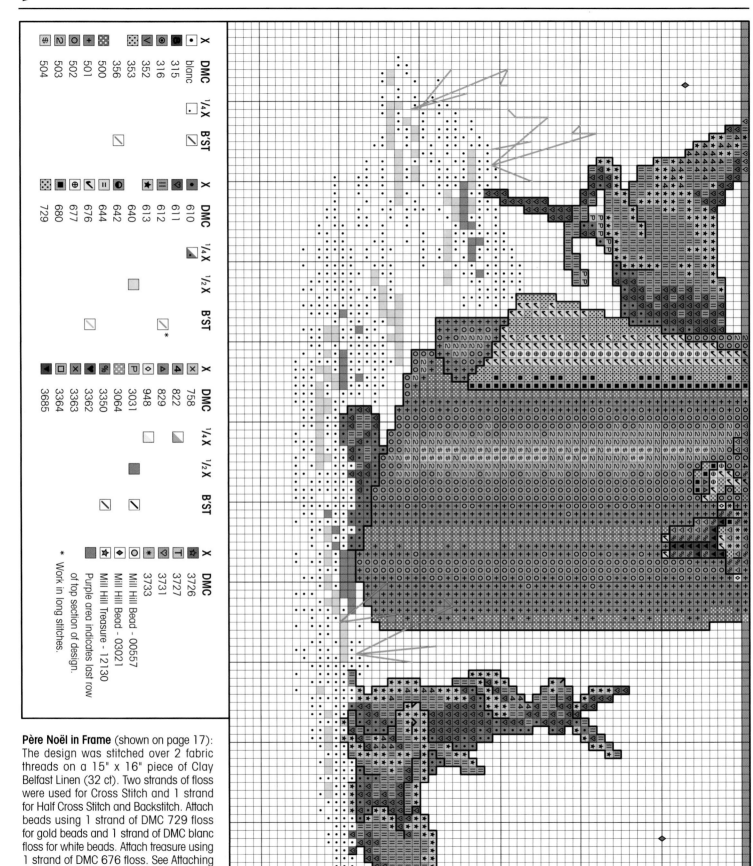

X	·	¼X		B'ST		DMC
⊞	·	·				blanc
▨				◿		315
◨						316
◪						352
◡						353
⊙						356
◩						500
⊡						501
◯						502
✛						503
⊠						504

X			¼X	½X	B'ST		DMC
▨							610
◼							611
⊕			◹				612
◣							613
‖							640
◑							642
★				◻			644
‖						◿	676
◣					*		677
●							680
							729

X			¼X	½X	B'ST		DMC
◀			◹				758
▢							822
✕							829
◀							948
◳							3031
◌				◼			3064
P							3350
◇						◿	3362
◢							3363
4					◿		3364
✕							3685

X						DMC
◼	★	◆	◯	✴	◀	3726
				⊤		3727
				✿		3731
						3733

Mill Hill Bead - 00557
Mill Hill Bead - 03021
Mill Hill Treasure - 12130

Purple area indicates last row
of top section of design.

* Work in long stitches.

Père Noël in Frame (shown on page 17):
The design was stitched over 2 fabric
threads on a 15" x 16" piece of Clay
Belfast Linen (32 ct). Two strands of floss
were used for Cross Stitch and 1 strand
for Half Cross Stitch and Backstitch. Attach
beads using 1 strand of DMC 729 floss
for gold beads and 1 strand of DMC blanc
floss for white beads. Attach treasure using
1 strand of DMC 676 floss. See Attaching
Beads, page 96. It was custom framed.

Needlework adaptation by Carol Emmer.

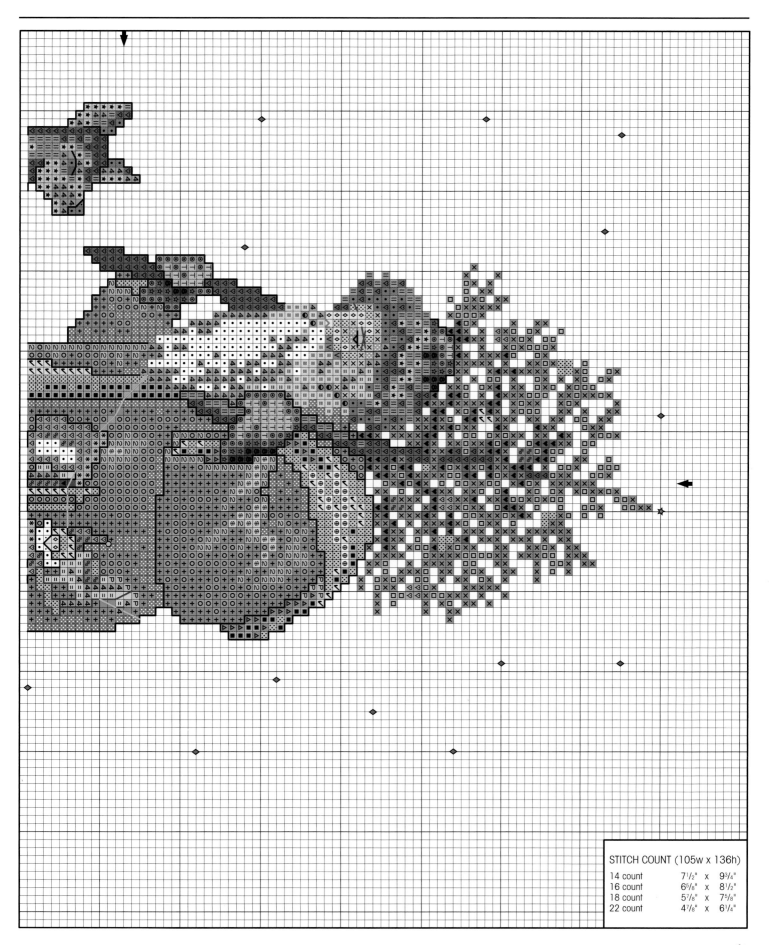

STITCH COUNT (105w x 136h)

14 count	7½"	x	9¾"
16 count	6⅝"	x	8½"
18 count	5⅞"	x	7⅝"
22 count	4⅞"	x	6¼"

with the christkindl

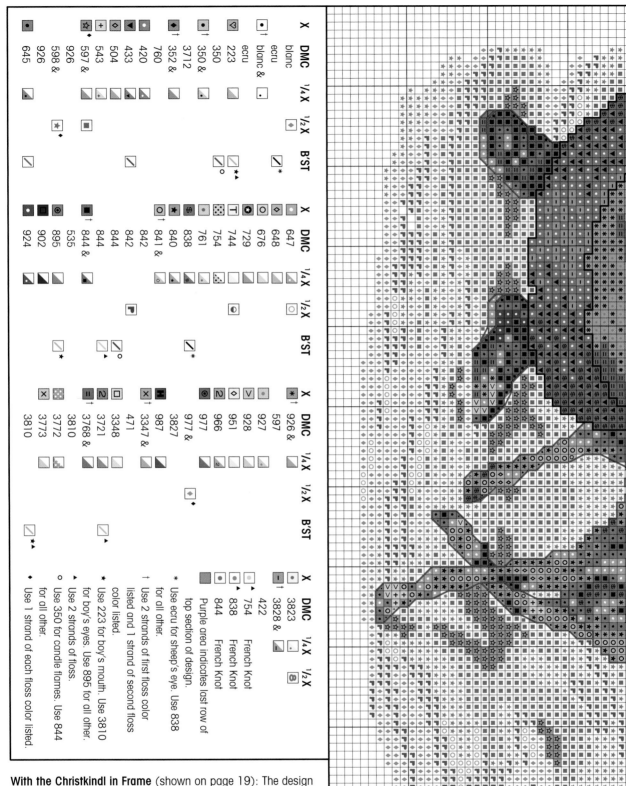

Color Key

X	DMC	1/4X	1/2X	B'ST
	blanc			
	ecru			
	blanc &			
	ecru			
	223			
	350			
	350 &			
	3712			
	352 &			
	760			
	504			
	433			
	420			
	760			
	597 &			
	543			
	597 &			
	926			
	598 &			
	926			
	645			

X	DMC	1/4X	1/2X	B'ST
	647			
	648			
	676			
	729			
	744			
	754			
	761			
	838			
	840			
	841 &			
	842			
	842			
	842			
	844			
	844			
	844			
	895			
	902			
	924			

X	DMC	1/4X	1/2X	B'ST
	926 &			
	597			
	927			
	928			
	951			
	966			
	977			
	977 &			
	3827			
	987			
	3347 &			
	3348			
	3721			
	3768 &			
	3810			
	3772			
	3773			
	3810			

X	DMC	1/4X	1/2X	
	3823			
	3828 &			
	422			
	754			French Knot
	838			French Knot
	844			French Knot

Purple area indicates last row of top section of design.

* Use ecru for sheep's eye. Use 838 for all other.

† Use 2 strands of first floss color listed and 1 strand of second floss color listed.

★ Use 223 for boy's eyes. Use 3810 for boy's mouth. Use 895 for all other.

▶ Use 2 strands of floss.

○ Use 350 for candle flames. Use 844 for all other.

◆ Use 1 strand of each floss color listed.

With the Christkindl in Frame (shown on page 19): The design was stitched over 2 fabric threads on a 15" x 17" piece of Antique Ivory Cashel Linen® (28 ct). Three strands of floss were used for Cross Stitch, 2 strands for Half Cross Stitch, and 1 strand for Backstitch and French Knots, unless otherwise noted in the color key. It was custom framed.

Needlework adaptation by Sandy Orton.

KOOLER DESIGN STUDIO

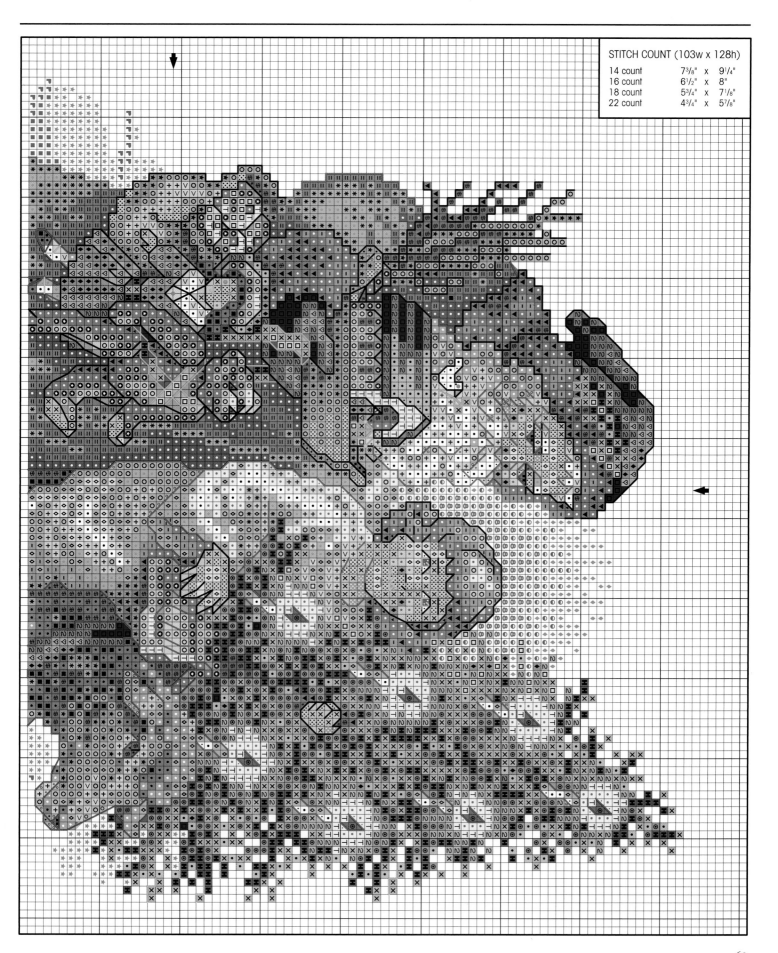

STITCH COUNT (103w x 128h)

14 count	7³/₈" x	9¹/₄"
16 count	6¹/₂" x	8"
18 count	5³/₄" x	7¹/₈"
22 count	4³/₄" x	5⁷/₈"

GRANDFATHER FROST

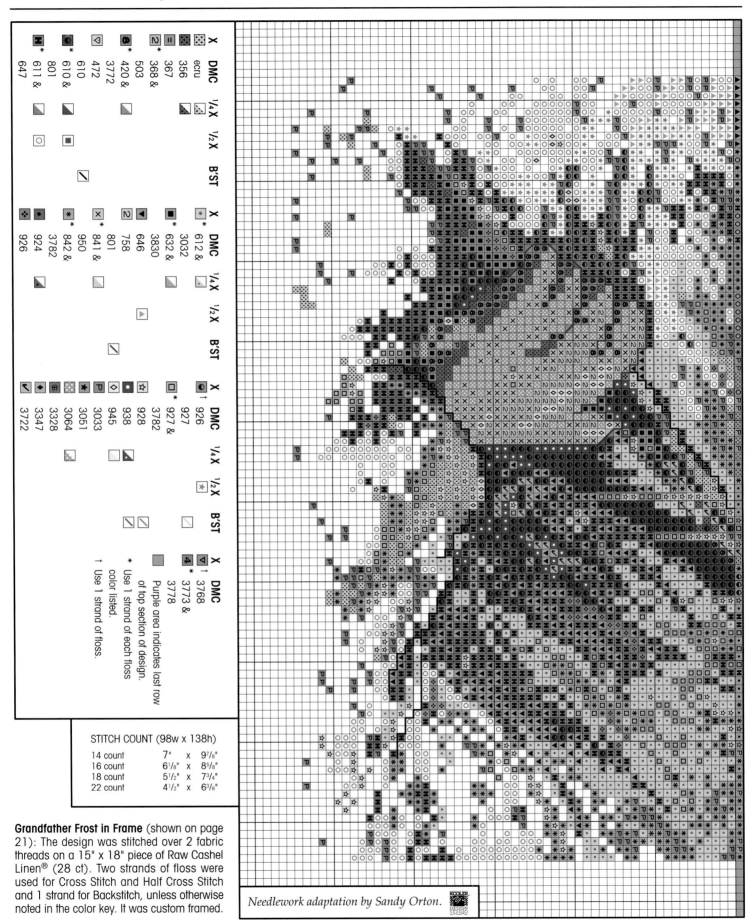

X			¼X	½X	B'ST	DMC
						ecru
						356
						367
						368 &
						503
						420 &
						472
						3772
						610
						610 &
						801
						611 &
						647

X			¼X	½X	B'ST	DMC
						612 &
						3032
						632 &
						3830
						646
						758
						801
						841 &
						950
						842 &
						3782
						924
						926

X			¼X	½X	B'ST	DMC
						926
						927
						927 &
						3782
						928
						938
						945
						3033
						3051
						3064
						3328
						3347
						3722

X			DMC
		†	3768
		4	3773 &
			3778

Purple area indicates last row of top section of design.

* Use 1 strand of each floss color listed.

† Use 1 strand of floss.

STITCH COUNT (98w x 138h)

14 count	7"	x	9⅞"
16 count	6⅛"	x	8⅝"
18 count	5½"	x	7¾"
22 count	4½"	x	6⅜"

Grandfather Frost in Frame (shown on page 21): The design was stitched over 2 fabric threads on a 15" x 18" piece of Raw Cashel Linen® (28 ct). Two strands of floss were used for Cross Stitch and Half Cross Stitch and 1 strand for Backstitch, unless otherwise noted in the color key. It was custom framed.

Needlework adaptation by Sandy Orton.

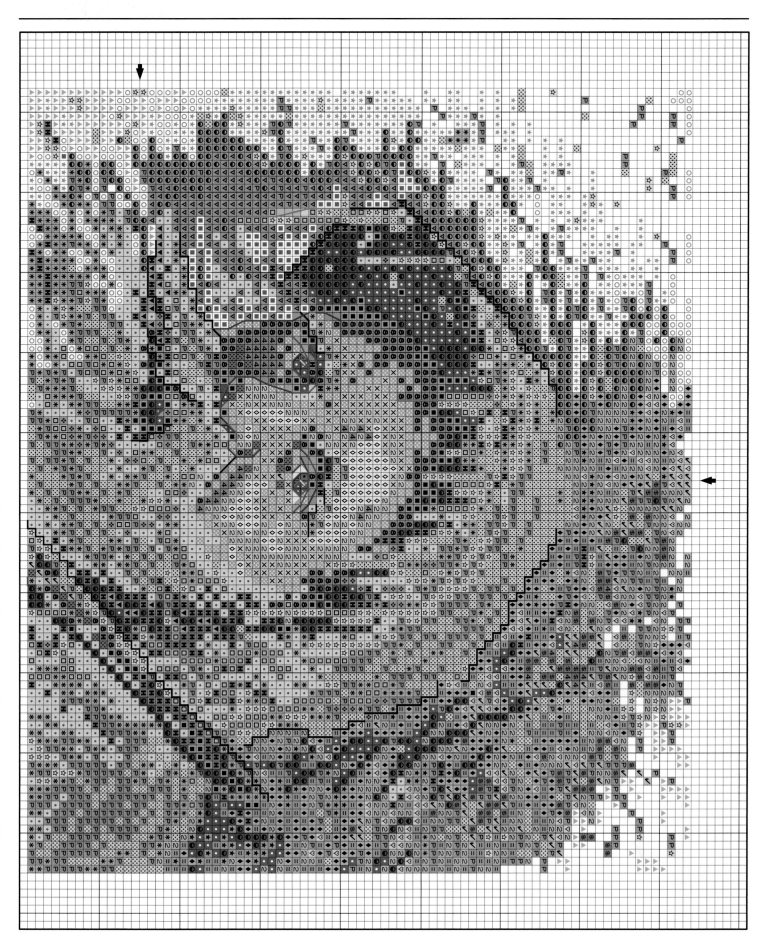

WEIHNACHTSMANN

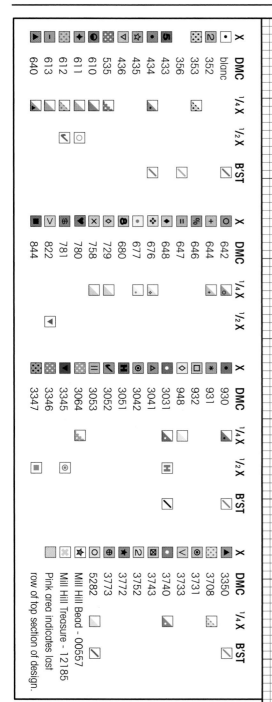

Weihnachtsmann in Frame (shown on page 23): The design was stitched over 2 fabric threads on a 15" x 18" piece of Misty Blue Quaker Cloth (28 ct). Two strands of floss were used for Cross Stitch and 1 strand for Half Cross Stitch and Backstitch. Attach beads and treasure using 1 strand of DMC 729 floss. See Attaching Beads, page 96. It was custom framed.

Needlework adaptation by Carol Emmer.

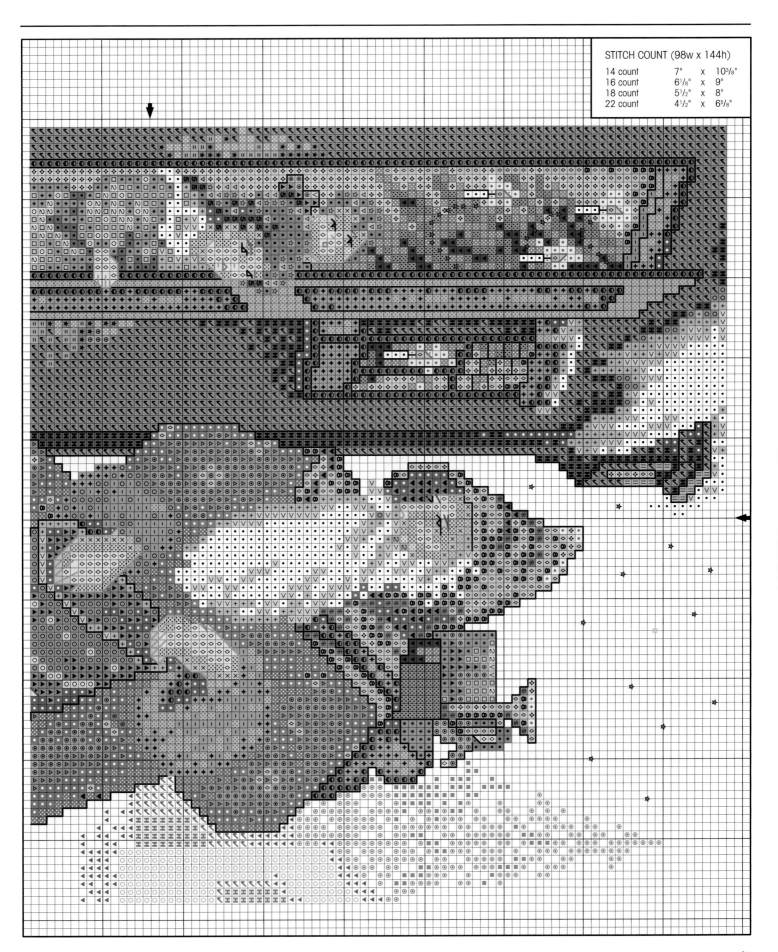

STITCH COUNT (98w x 144h)

14 count	7"	x	10³/₈"
16 count	6¹/₈"	x	9"
18 count	5¹/₂"	x	8"
22 count	4¹/₂"	x	6⁵/₈"

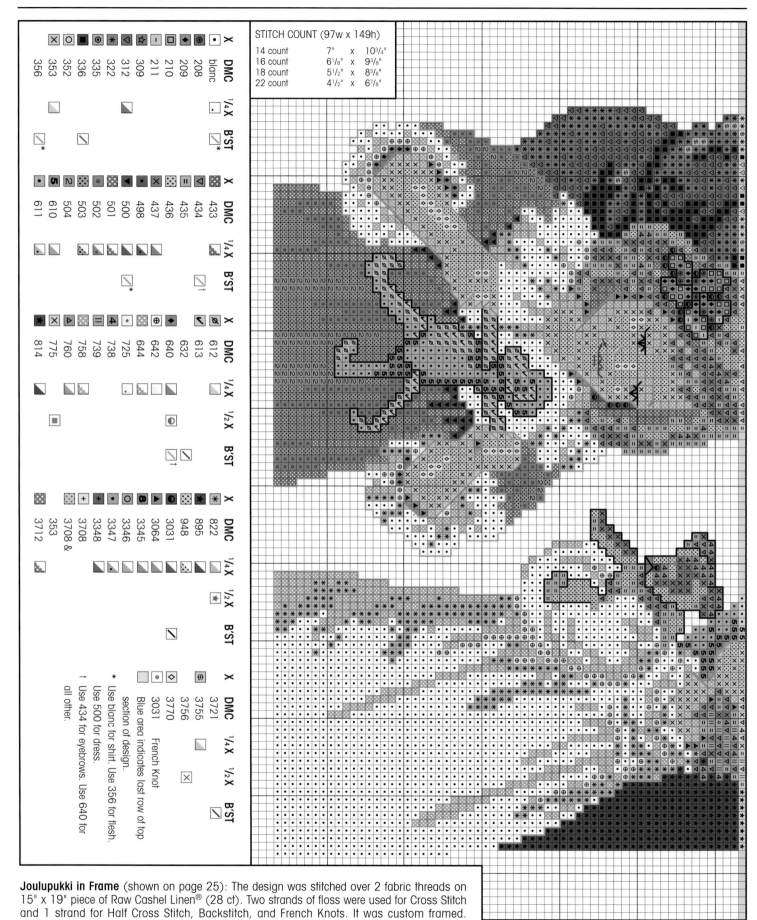

STITCH COUNT (97w x 149h)

14 count	7" x 10¾"
16 count	6⅛" x 9⅜"
18 count	5½" x 8⅜"
22 count	4½" x 6⅞"

Color Key (DMC):

X / DMC / ¼X / B'ST

356, 353, 352, 336, 335, 322, 312, 309, 211, 210, 209, 208, blanc

611, 610, 504, 503, 502, 501, 500, 498, 437, 436, 435, 434, 433

814, 775, 760, 758, 739, 738, 725, 644, 642, 640, 632, 613, 612

3712, 353, 3708, 3708 &, 3348, 3347, 3346, 3345, 3064, 3031, 948, 895, 822

3721, 3755, 3756, 3770, 3031

French Knot

* Use blanc for shirt. Use 356 for flesh.
† Use 434 for eyebrows. Use 640 for all other.

Blue area indicates last row of top section of design.
Use blanc for dress. Use 500 for...

Joulupukki in Frame (shown on page 25): The design was stitched over 2 fabric threads on 15" x 19" piece of Raw Cashel Linen® (28 ct). Two strands of floss were used for Cross Stitch and 1 strand for Half Cross Stitch, Backstitch, and French Knots. It was custom framed.

Needlework adaptation by Carol Emmer.

FATHER CHRISTMAS IN CRIMSON

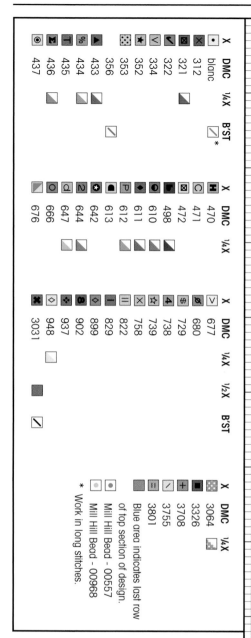

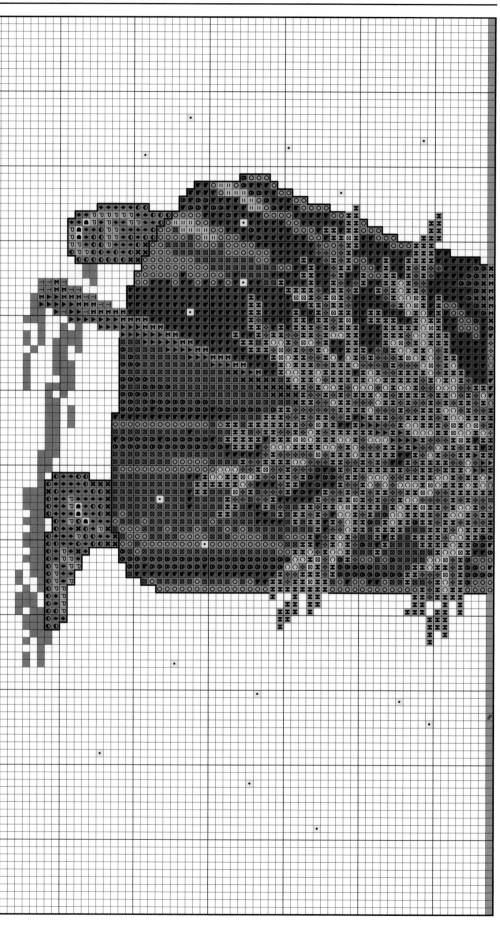

Father Christmas in Crimson in Frame (shown on page 27): The design was stitched over 2 fabric threads on a 15" x 19" piece of Raw Cashel Linen® (28 ct). Two strands of floss were used for Cross Stitch and 1 strand for Half Cross Stitch and Backstitch. Attach beads using 1 strand of DMC 676 floss for gold beads and 1 strand of DMC 666 floss for red beads. See Attaching Beads, page 96. It was custom framed.

Needlework adaptation by Carol Emmer.

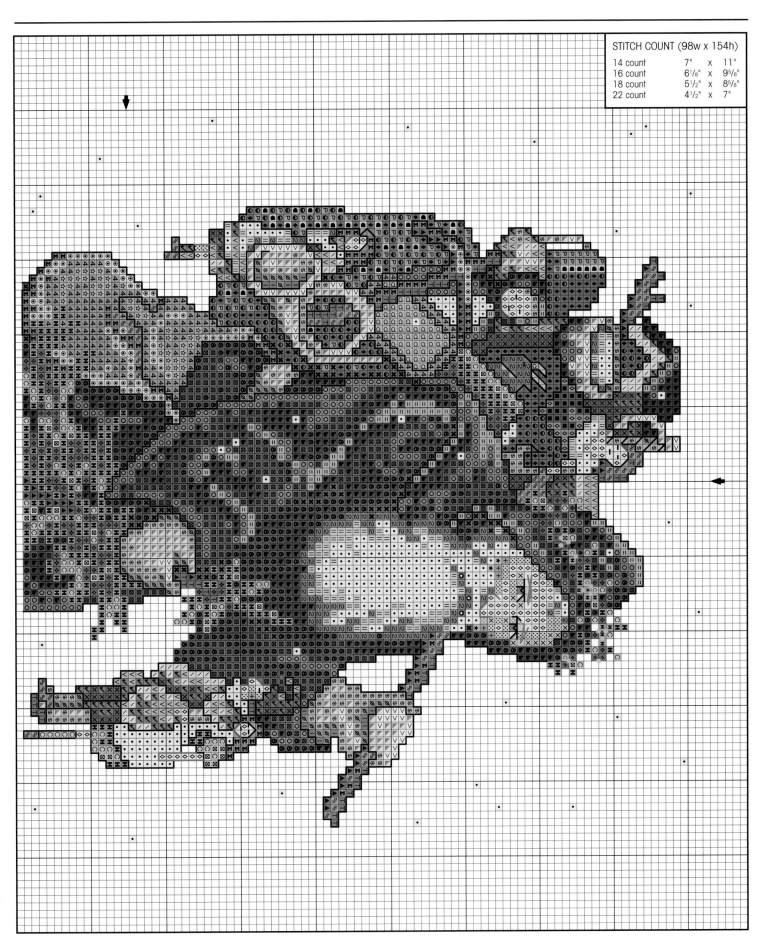

STITCH COUNT (98w x 154h)

14 count	7"	x	11"
16 count	6¹/₈"	x	9⁵/₈"
18 count	5¹/₂"	x	8⁵/₈"
22 count	4¹/₂"	x	7"

JOLLY OLD ELF

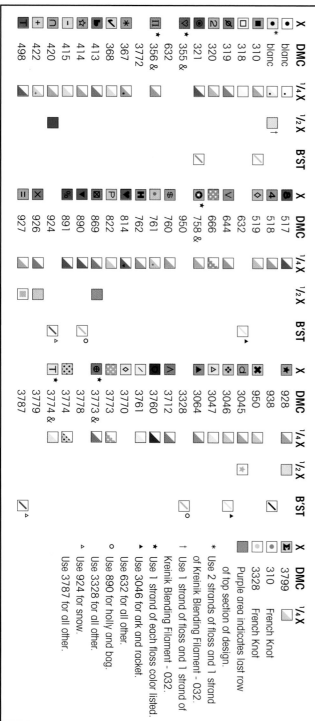

Jolly Old Elf in Frame (shown on page 29): The design was stitched over 2 fabric threads on a 15" x 18" piece of Misty Blue Quaker Cloth (28 ct). Two strands of floss were used for Cross Stitch and 1 strand for Backstitch and French Knots, unless otherwise noted in the color key. It was custom framed.

Needlework adaptation by Donna Vermillion Giampa.

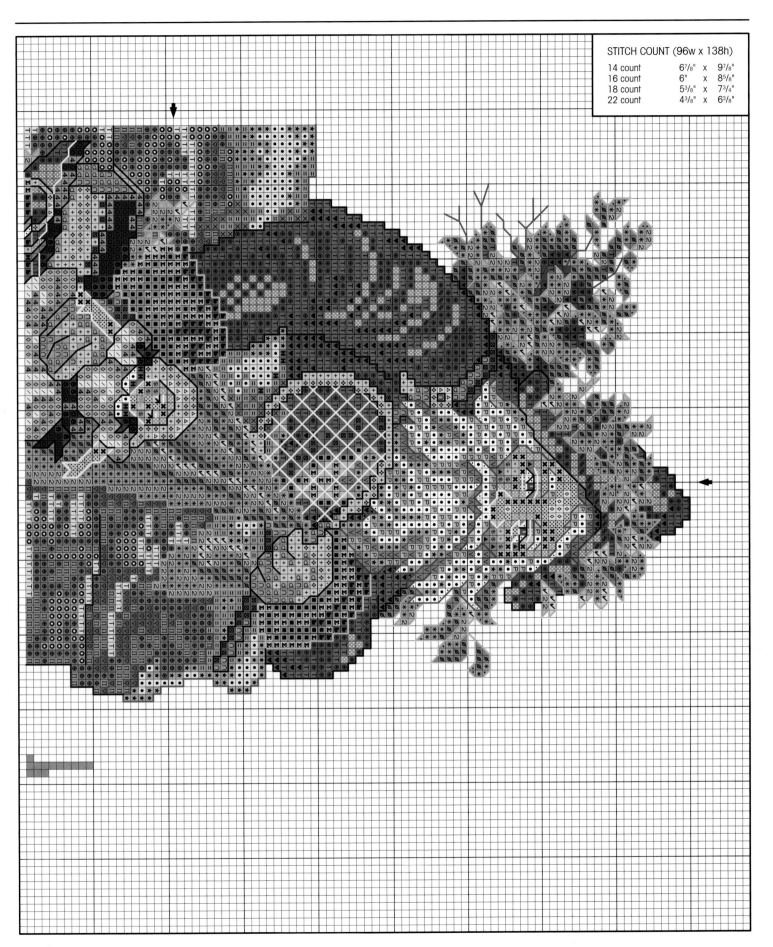

STITCH COUNT (96w x 138h)

14 count	6⁷⁄₈" x	9⁷⁄₈"
16 count	6" x	8⁵⁄₈"
18 count	5³⁄₈" x	7³⁄₄"
22 count	4³⁄₈" x	6³⁄₈"

santa's workshop

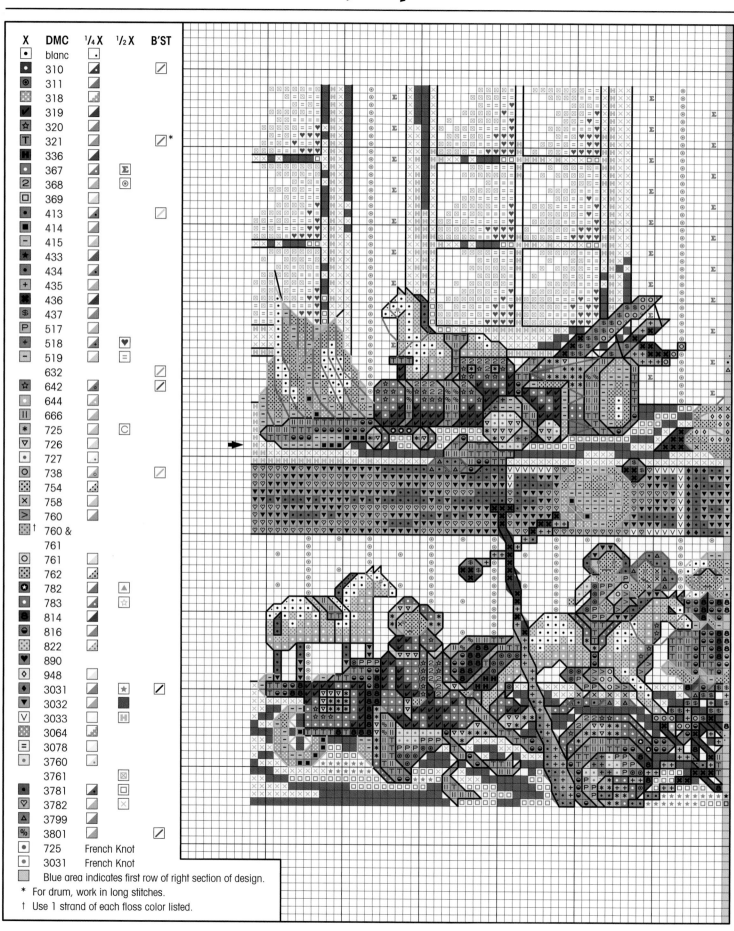

X	DMC	¼X	½X	B'ST
•	blanc	•		
●	310			/
◉	311			
▦	318			
✔	319			
☆	320			
T	321			/*
⊞	336			
⊡	367		Σ	
2	368		◉	
▢	369			
•	413			/
■	414			
–	415			
★	433			
•	434			
+	435			
✖	436			
$	437			
P	517			
✚	518		♥	
–	519		=	
	632			/
☆	642			/
⊡	644			
‖	666			
✻	725		C	
▽	726			
•	727			
O	738			/
⊞	754			
X	758			
➤	760			
⊞ †	760 &			
	761			
O	761			
⊞	762			
✪	782		▲	
⊡	783		☆	
▨	814			
●	816			
⊞	822			
♥	890			
◇	948			
◆	3031		★	/
▼	3032		■	
V	3033		H	
⊞	3064			
=	3078			
⊡	3760	•		
	3761		⊠	
●	3781		▢	
♡	3782		X	
△	3799			
%	3801			/
•	725	French Knot		
•	3031	French Knot		

Blue area indicates first row of right section of design.

* For drum, work in long stitches.

† Use 1 strand of each floss color listed.

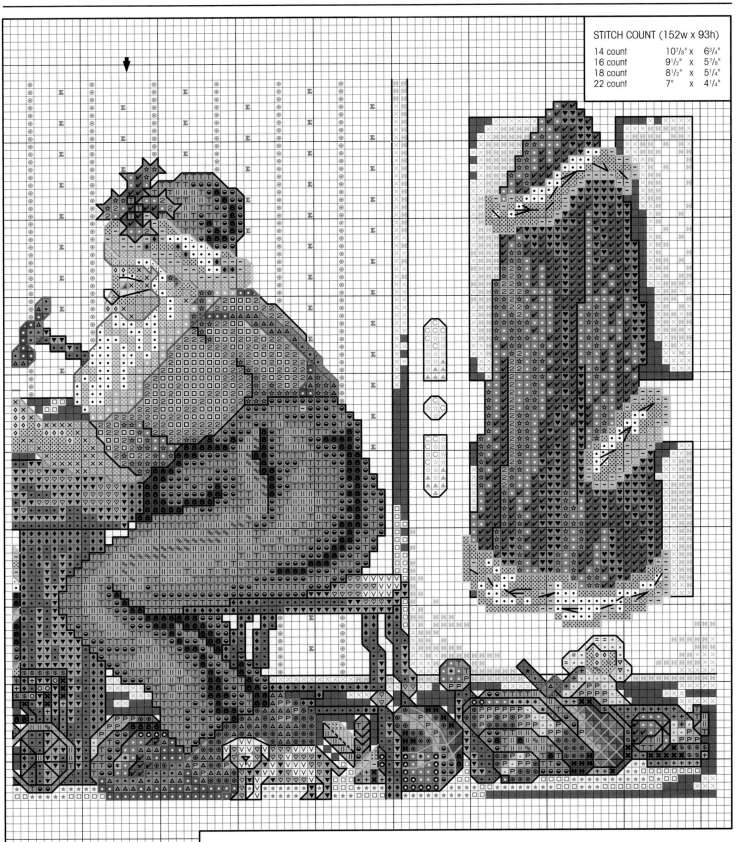

STITCH COUNT (152w x 93h)

14 count	10⅞"	x	6¾"
16 count	9½"	x	5⅞"
18 count	8½"	x	5¼"
22 count	7"	x	4¼"

Santa's Workshop in Frame (shown on page 31): The design was stitched over 2 fabric threads on a 19" x 15" piece of Cream Cashel Linen® (28 ct). Two strands of floss were used for Cross Stitch and 1 strand for Half Cross Stitch, Backstitch, and French Knots. It was custom framed.

Needlework adaptation by Donna Vermillion Giampa.

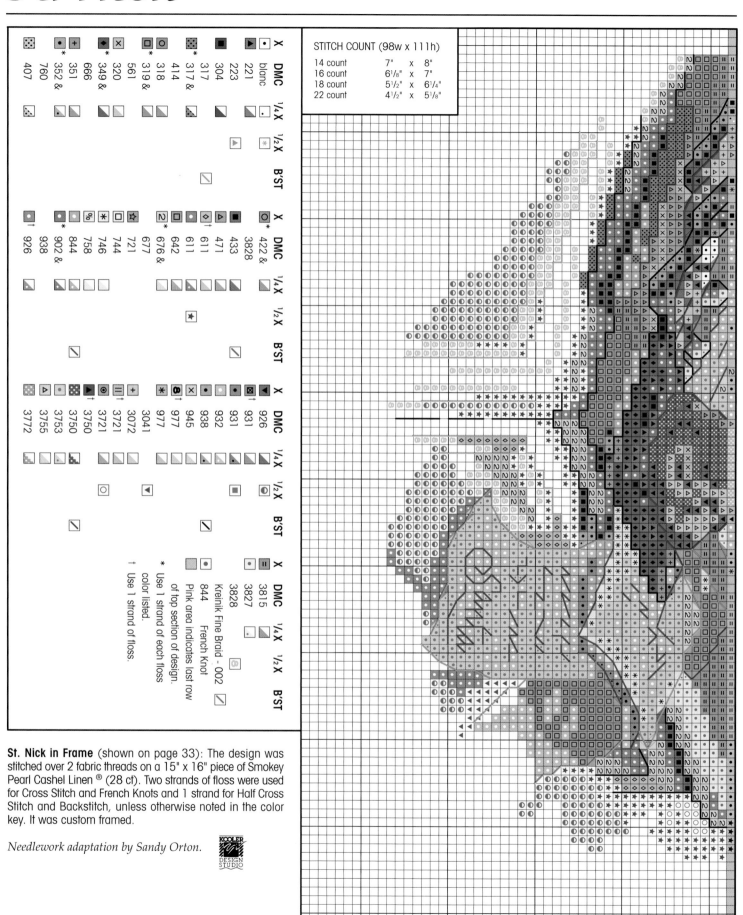

STITCH COUNT (98w x 111h)

14 count	7"	x	8"	
16 count	6 1/8"	x	7"	
18 count	5 1/2"	x	6 1/4"	
22 count	4 1/2"	x	5 1/8"	

X	DMC	1/4X	1/2X	B'ST
	blanc			
	221			
	223			
	304			
	317			
	317 &			
	414			
	318			
	319 &			
	320			
	561			
	349 &			
	666			
	351			
	352 &			
	760			
	407			

X	DMC	1/4X	1/2X	B'ST
	422 &			
	3828			
	433			
	471			
	611			
	611			
	642			
	676 &			
	677			
	721			
	744			
	746			
	758			
	844			
	902 &			
	938			
	926			

X	DMC	1/4X	1/2X	B'ST
	926			
	931			
	931			
	932			
	938			
	945			
	977			
	977			
	3041			
	3072			
	3721			
	3721			
	3750			
	3750			
	3753			
	3755			
	3772			

X	DMC	1/4X	1/2X	B'ST
	3815			
	3827			
	3828			
	844 French Knot			
	Kreinik Fine Braid - 002			

* Use 1 strand of each floss color listed.

Pink area indicates last row of top section of design.

† Use 1 strand of floss.

St. Nick in Frame (shown on page 33): The design was stitched over 2 fabric threads on a 15" x 16" piece of Smokey Pearl Cashel Linen ® (28 ct). Two strands of floss were used for Cross Stitch and French Knots and 1 strand for Half Cross Stitch and Backstitch, unless otherwise noted in the color key. It was custom framed.

Needlework adaptation by Sandy Orton.

KOOLER DESIGN STUDIO

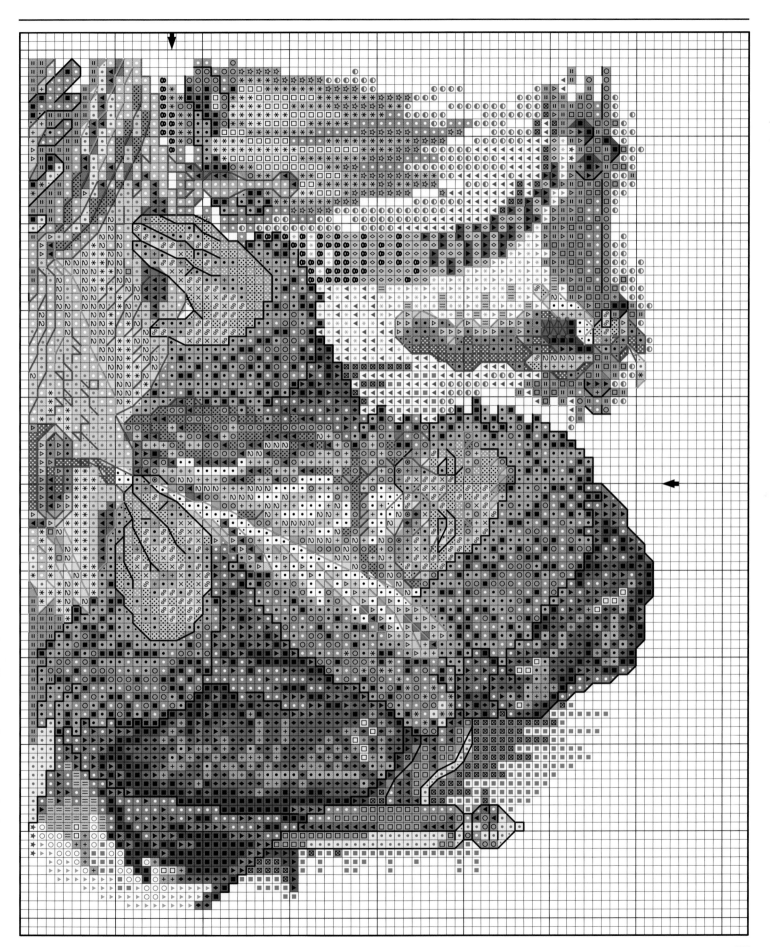

VICTORIAN SANTA

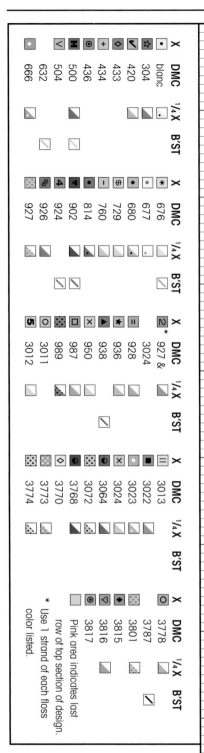

Victorian Santa in Frame (shown on page 35): The design was stitched over 2 fabric threads on a 15" x 18" piece of Dirty Cashel Linen® (28 ct). Two strands of floss were used for Cross Stitch and 1 strand for Backstitch. It was custom framed.

Needlework adaptation by Donna Vermillion Giampa.

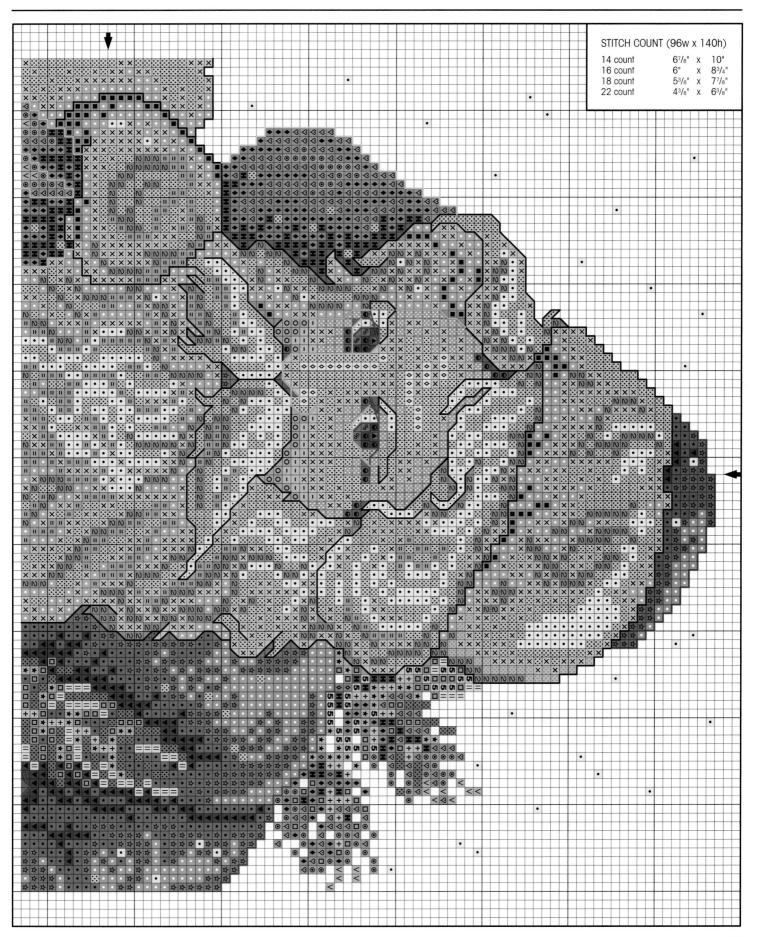

STITCH COUNT (96w x 140h)

14 count	6⁷/₈" x	10"
16 count	6" x	8³/₄"
18 count	5³/₈" x	7⁷/₈"
22 count	4³/₈" x	6³/₈"

YULETIDE PATRIOT

Needlework adaptation by Carol Emmer.

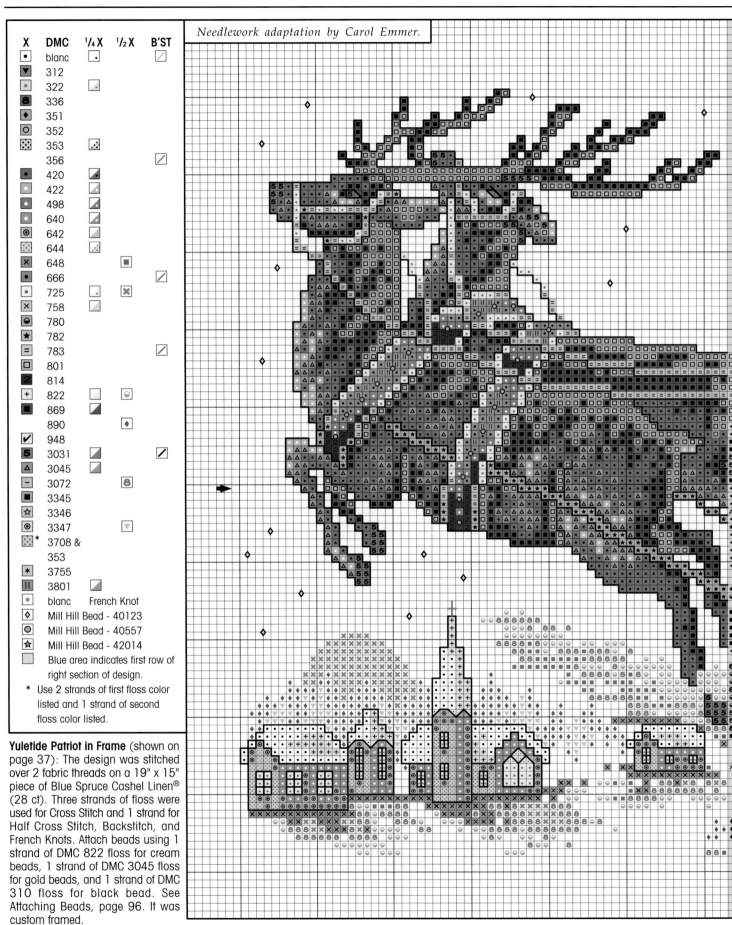

X	DMC	¼ X	½ X	B'ST
•	blanc	•		
▼	312			
•	322	•		
❻	336			
◆	351			
○	352			
▦	353	▦		
	356			/
▪	420		◢	
▫	422		◢	
◉	498		◢	
▪	640		◢	
◎	642		◢	
▦	644		◢	
✕	648		▪	
●	666			/
•	725	•	✕	
✕	758		◢	
◓	780			
★	782			
=	783			/
▢	801			
❷	814			
+	822	▫	◎	
▪	869		◢	
	890		◆	
✔	948			
❺	3031	◢		/
△	3045	◢		
−	3072		❻	
▪	3345			
☆	3346			
◉	3347		▽	
▦*	3708 &			
	353			
✳	3755			
‖	3801	◢		
◉	blanc	French Knot		
◇	Mill Hill Bead - 40123			
○	Mill Hill Bead - 40557			
★	Mill Hill Bead - 42014			
▨	Blue area indicates first row of right section of design.			

* Use 2 strands of first floss color listed and 1 strand of second floss color listed.

Yuletide Patriot in Frame (shown on page 37): The design was stitched over 2 fabric threads on a 19" x 15" piece of Blue Spruce Cashel Linen® (28 ct). Three strands of floss were used for Cross Stitch and 1 strand for Half Cross Stitch, Backstitch, and French Knots. Attach beads using 1 strand of DMC 822 floss for cream beads, 1 strand of DMC 3045 floss for gold beads, and 1 strand of DMC 310 floss for black bead. See Attaching Beads, page 96. It was custom framed.

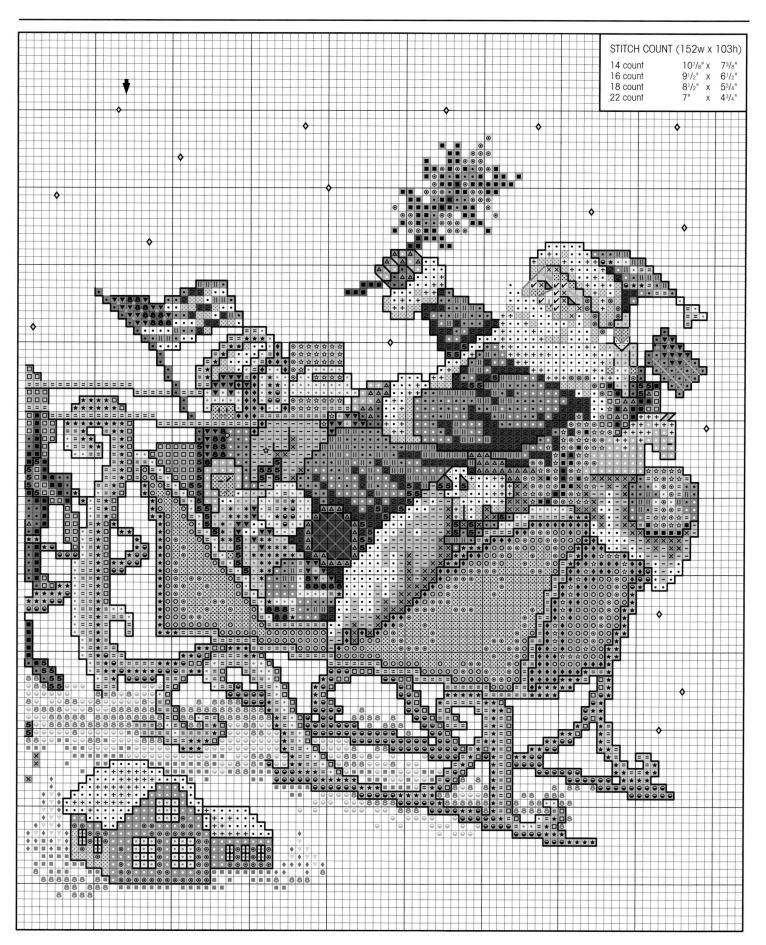

STITCH COUNT (152w x 103h)

14 count	10⁷/₈" x	7³/₈"
16 count	9¹/₂" x	6¹/₂"
18 count	8¹/₂" x	5³/₄"
22 count	7" x	4³/₄"

MERRY OLD SANTA

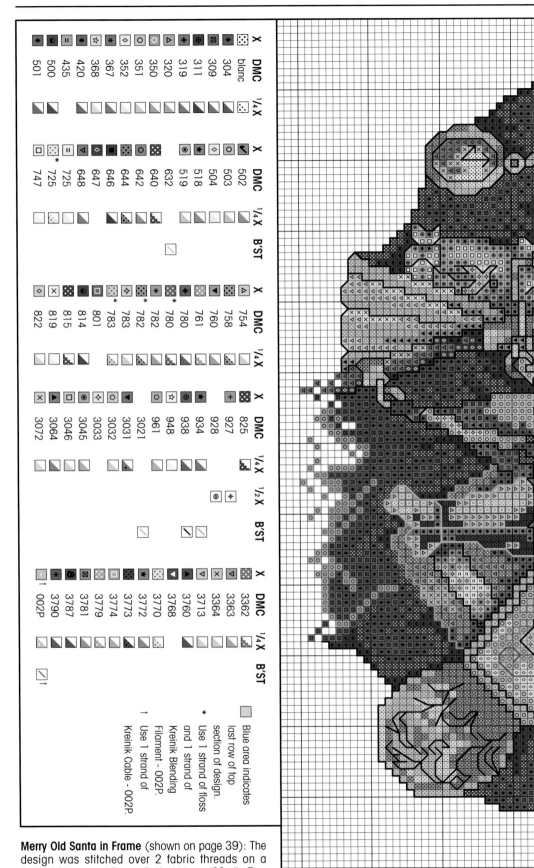

X	DMC	¼X
◆	501	
◑	500	◨
‖	435	◨
◆	420	◨
☆	368	◨
✳	367	◨
◐	352	◨
○	351	◨
◉	350	◨
▷	320	◨
◆	319	◨
⊕	311	◨
⊠	309	◨
◆	304	◨
	blanc	◨

X	DMC	¼X	B'ST
▢	502		
◪	503	◨	
‖	504	◨	
◀	518	◨	
■	519	◨	◹
◨	632	◨	
◑	640		
◉	642	◨	
◈	644	◨	
○	646	◨	
	647	◨	
	648	◨	
*	725	◨	
	725	◨	
	747	◨	

X	DMC	¼X
◇	754	
✕	758	
◫	760	
◐	761	
◫	780	
◆	780	
✦	782	
✳	782	
	783	
*	783	
◆	801	◨
◨	814	◨
	815	◨
	819	◨
	822	◨

X	DMC	¼X	½X	B'ST
✕	825	◨		
▶	927	◨		
▢	928			
◉	934			
◇	938	◨		
○	948	◨		
	961			
◇	3021			
☆	3031			◹
⊕	3032		◉	
✳	3033		✦	
+	3045			
	3046	◨		
	3064	◨		
	3072	◨		

X	DMC	¼X	B'ST
▢	3362	◨	
*	3363	◑	
◑	3364	◨	
⊠	3713	◨	
	3760	◨	
◀	3768	◨	
	3770	◨	
✕	3772	◨	
◀	3773	◨	
	3774	◨	
★	3779	◨	
◨	3781	◨	
◈	3787	◨	
▦	3790	◨	
	002P		◹†

▨ Blue area indicates last row of top section of design.

* Use 1 strand of floss and 1 strand of Kreinik Blending Filament - 002P.

† Use 1 strand of Kreinik Cable - 002P.

Merry Old Santa in Frame (shown on page 39): The design was stitched over 2 fabric threads on a 15" x 18" piece of Cream Belfast Linen (32 ct). Two strands of floss were used for Cross Stitch and 1 strand for Half Cross Stitch and Backstitch. It was custom framed.

STITCH COUNT (116w x 162h)

14 count	8³/₈"	x	11⁵/₈"
16 count	7¹/₄"	x	10¹/₈"
18 count	6¹/₂"	x	9"
22 count	5³/₈"	x	7³/₈"

Needlework adaptation by Donna Vermillion Giampa.

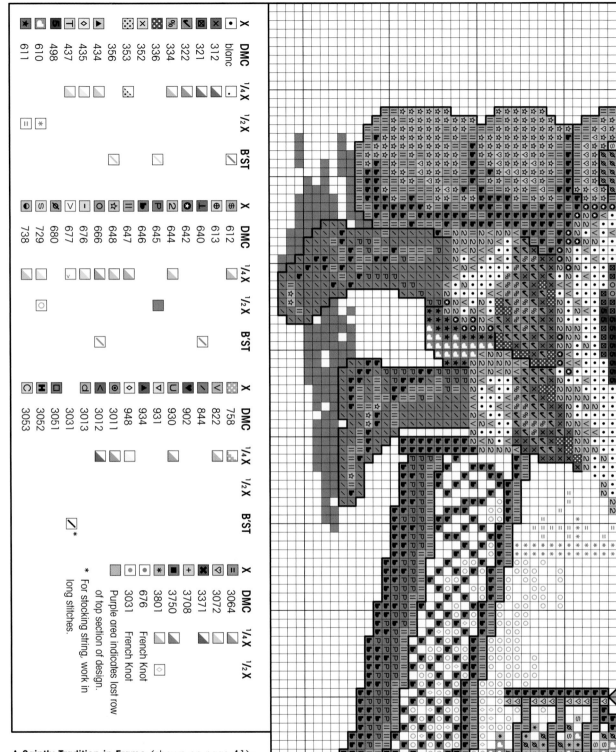

A Saintly Tradition in Frame (shown on page 41): The design was stitched over 2 fabric threads on a 14" x 18" piece of Raw Cashel Linen® (28 ct). Two strands of floss were used for Cross Stitch and 1 strand for Half Cross Stitch, Backstitch, and French Knots. It was custom framed.

Needlework adaptation by Carol Emmer.

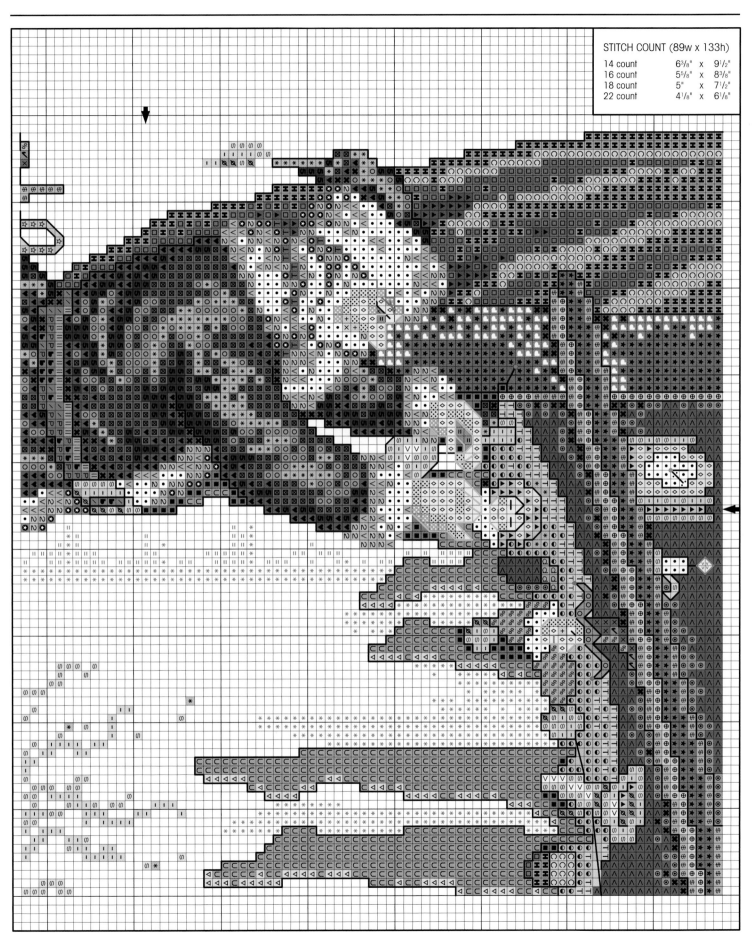

STITCH COUNT (89w x 133h)

14 count	6³⁄₈"	x	9¹⁄₂"
16 count	5⁵⁄₈"	x	8³⁄₈"
18 count	5"	x	7¹⁄₂"
22 count	4¹⁄₈"	x	6¹⁄₈"

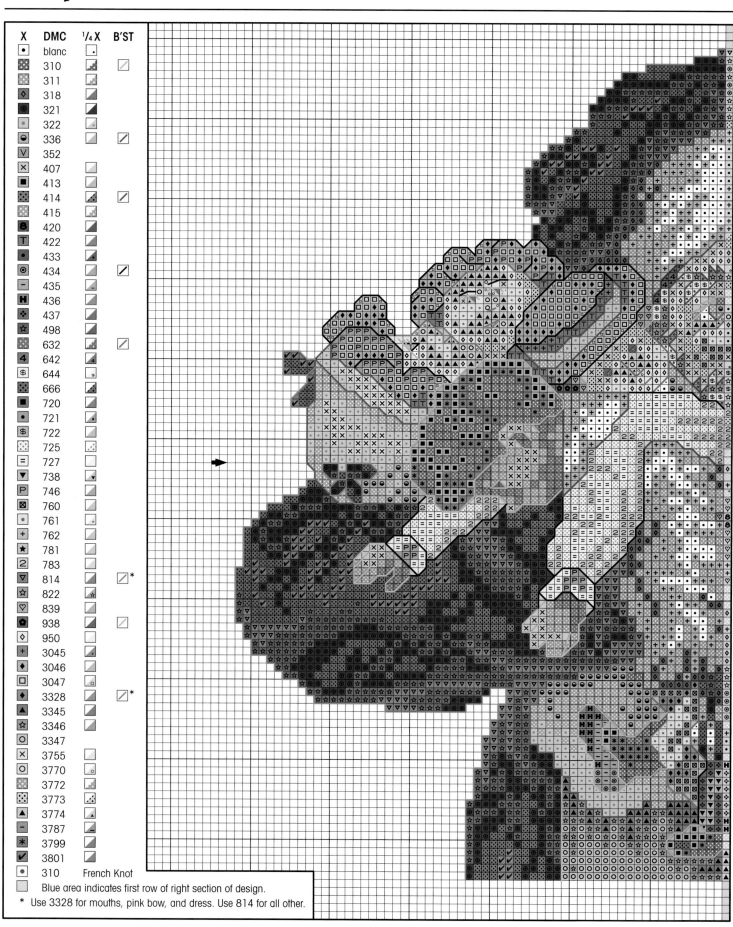

X	DMC	¼X	B'ST
•	blanc	•	
	310		◪
	311		
◇	318	◪	
◉	321	◪	
	322	◪	◪
⊖	336	◪	
V	352		
X	407	◪	
■	413		
	414	◪	◪
	415	◪	
8	420	◪	
T	422	◪	
	433	◪	
◉	434	◪	◪
–	435	◪	
H	436	◪	
	437	◪	
☆	498	◪	
	632	◪	◪
4	642	4	
$	644		
	666	◪	
■	720	◪	
•	721	◪	
$	722	◪	
	725		
=	727		
▼	738	◪	
P	746		
	760	◪	
•	761	•	
+	762	◪	
★	781	◪	
2	783	◪	
▽	814	◪	◪*
☆	822	◪	
♡	839	◪	
⬠	938	◪	◪
◇	950		
+	3045	4	
◆	3046	◪	
▢	3047	•	
◆	3328	◪	◪*
▲	3345	◪	
☆	3346	◪	
O	3347		
X	3755		
O	3770	•	
	3772		
	3773	◪	
▲	3774	▲	
–	3787	◪	
*	3799	◪	
✔	3801	◪	
⊙	310	French Knot	

Blue area indicates first row of right section of design.

* Use 3328 for mouths, pink bow, and dress. Use 814 for all other.

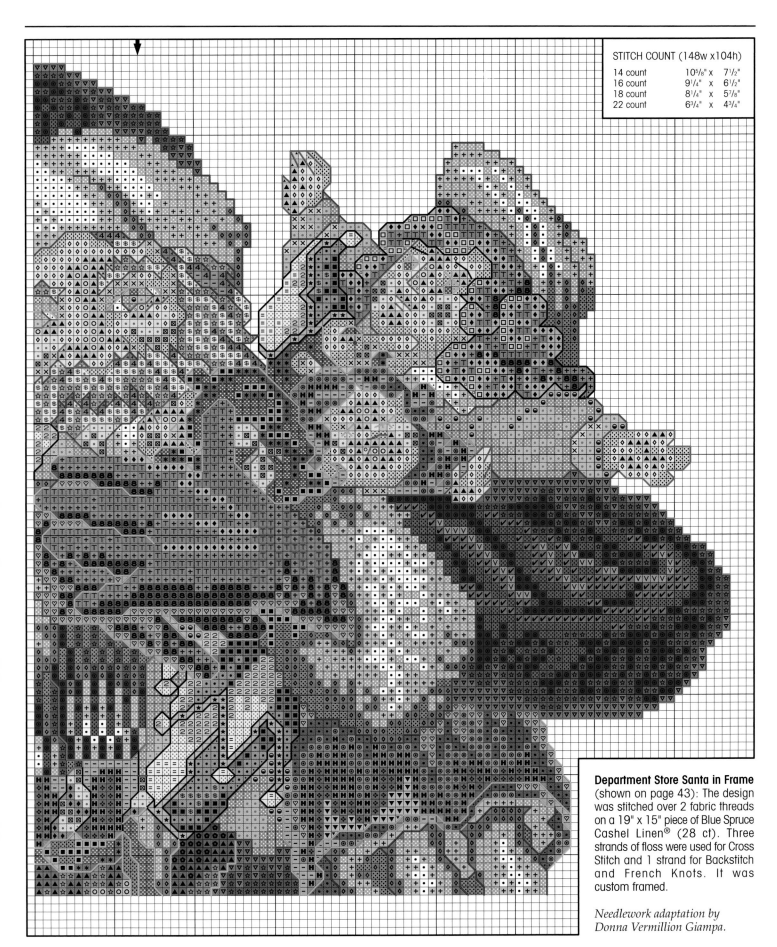

STITCH COUNT (148w x104h)

14 count	10⅝" x	7½"
16 count	9¼" x	6½"
18 count	8¼" x	5⅞"
22 count	6¾" x	4¾"

Department Store Santa in Frame
(shown on page 43): The design
was stitched over 2 fabric threads
on a 19" x 15" piece of Blue Spruce
Cashel Linen® (28 ct). Three
strands of floss were used for Cross
Stitch and 1 strand for Backstitch
and French Knots. It was
custom framed.

*Needlework adaptation by
Donna Vermillion Giampa.*

SINCERELY, SANTA

X	DMC	1/4X	B'ST
	blanc		*†
	356		
★	356 & 632		
★	407 & 356		
	434		*
	436		
	632		
	647		
	666		
	712		
	739		
	758		▲○
★	758 & 356		
★	758 & 407		
	817		
	822		
	838		○
	839		
	840		
	841		
	902		
	945		
	951		
	3328		
★	3328 & 822		
	3371		▲
	3770		
	5282 & 632		■

Grey area indicates last row of top section of design.

* Use blanc for glasses. Use 434 for beard.
† Use 3 strands of floss.
★ Use 1 strand of each floss color listed.
▲ Use 3371 for feather. Use 758 for all other.
○ Use 2 strands of floss.
■ Use 2 strands of first floss color listed and 1 strand of second floss color listed.

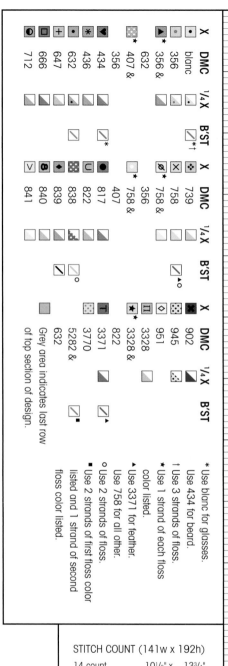

STITCH COUNT (141w x 192h)

14 count	10 1/8"	x	13 3/4"
16 count	8 7/8"	x	12"
18 count	7 7/8"	x	10 3/4"
22 count	6 1/2"	x	8 3/4"

Sincerely, Santa in Frame (shown on page 45): The design was stitched over 2 fabric threads on an 18" x 22" piece of Confederate Grey Cashel Linen® (28 ct). Two strands of floss were used for Cross Stitch and 1 strand for Backstitch, unless otherwise noted in the color key. It was custom framed.

© 1999, Ernie Norcia.
Exclusively represented by
Applejack Licensing International.

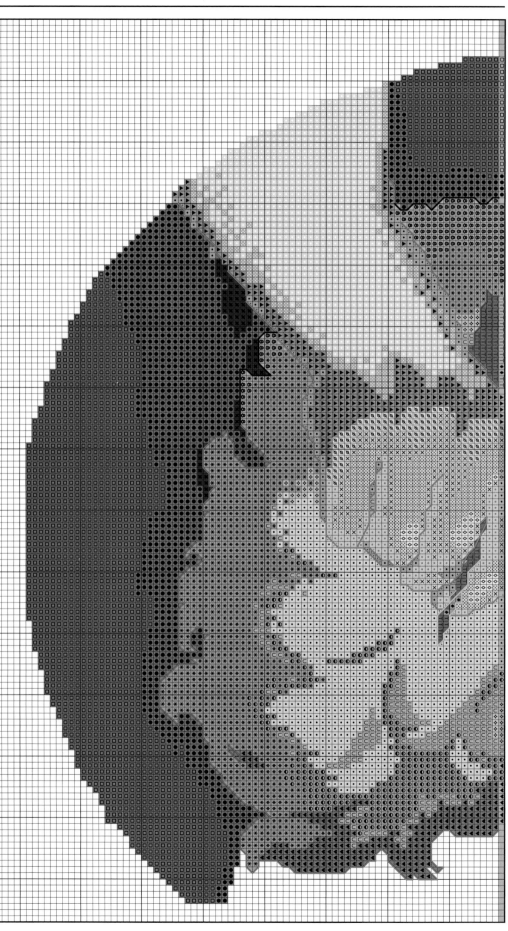

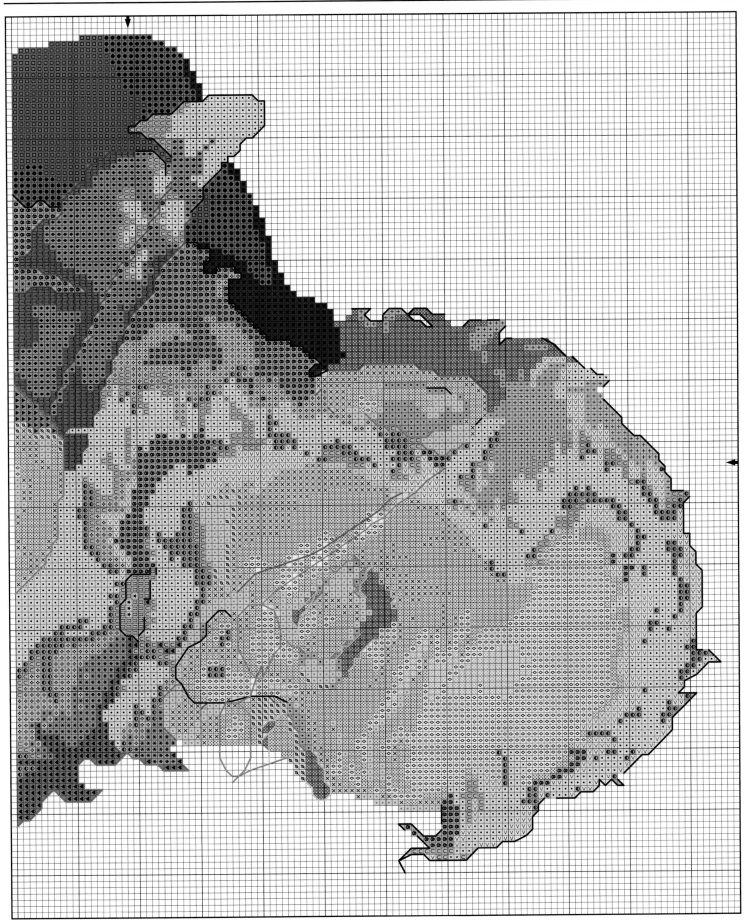

christmas patches

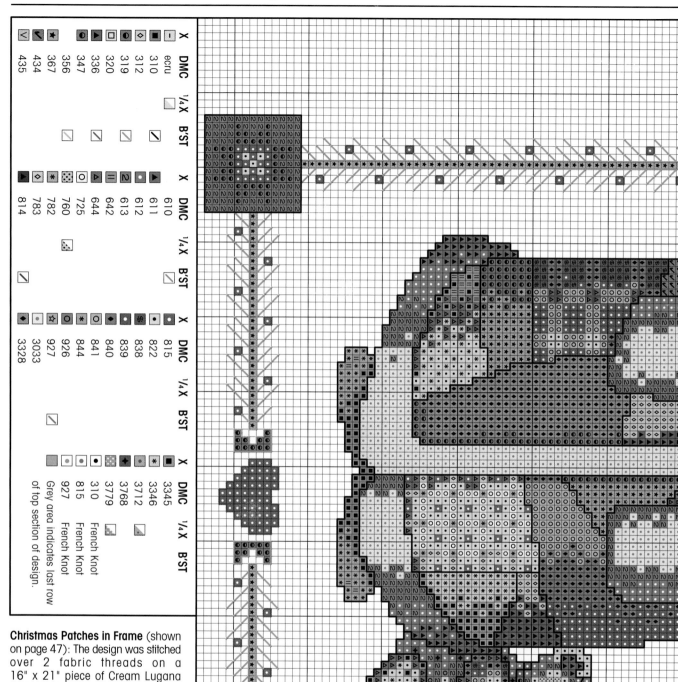

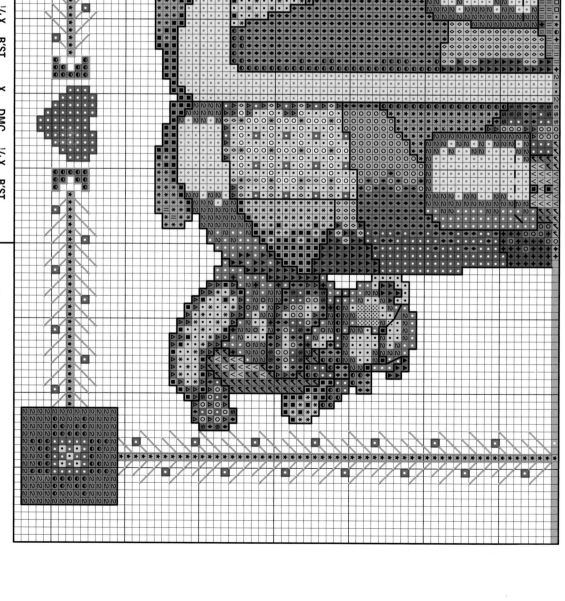

X	DMC	1/4X	B'ST
	ecru		
	310		
	312		
	319		
	320		
	336		
	347		
	356		
	367		
	434		
	435		

X	DMC	1/4X	B'ST
	610		
	611		
	612		
	613		
	642		
	644		
	725		
	760		
	782		
	783		
	814		

X	DMC	1/4X	B'ST
	815		
	822		
	838		
	839		
	840		
	841		
	844		
	926		
	927		
	3033		
	3328		

X	DMC	1/4X	B'ST
	3345		
	3346		
	3712		
	3768		
	3779		
	310 French Knot		
	815 French Knot		
	927 French Knot		

Grey area indicates last row of top section of design.

Christmas Patches in Frame (shown on page 47): The design was stitched over 2 fabric threads on a 16" x 21" piece of Cream Lugana (25 ct). Three strands of floss were used for Cross Stitch and 1 strand for Backstitch and French Knots. It was custom framed.

Design by Sandi Gore Evans. Needlework adaptation by Jane Chandler.

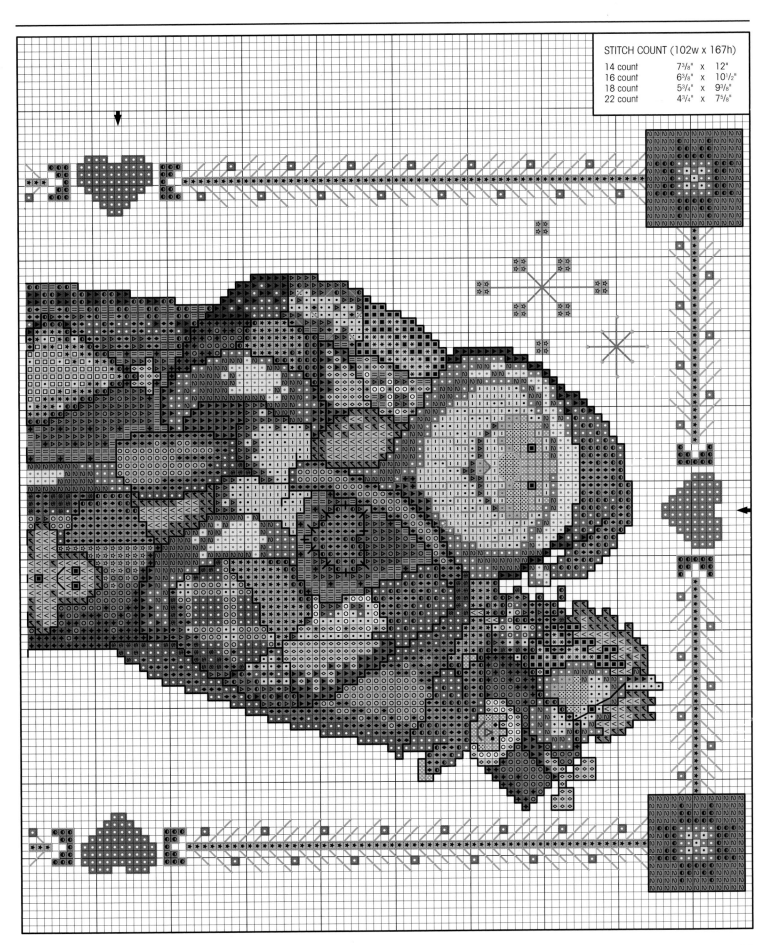

STITCH COUNT (102w x 167h)

14 count	7³⁄₈" x	12"
16 count	6³⁄₈" x	10¹⁄₂"
18 count	5³⁄₄" x	9³⁄₈"
22 count	4³⁄₄" x	7⁵⁄₈"

checking his list

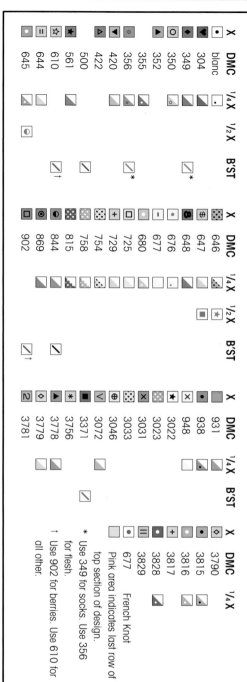

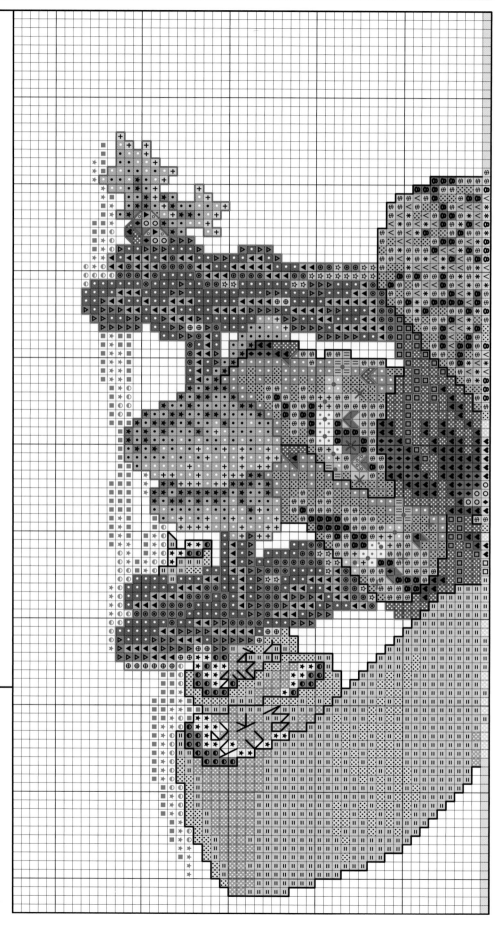

Checking His List in Frame (shown on page 49): The design was stitched over 2 fabric threads on a 16" x 18" piece of Antique White Lugana (25 ct). Three strands of floss were used for Cross Stitch and 1 strand for Half Cross Stitch, Backstitch, and French Knots. It was custom framed.

Design by Shirley Wilson.
Needlework adaptation by Nancy Dockter.

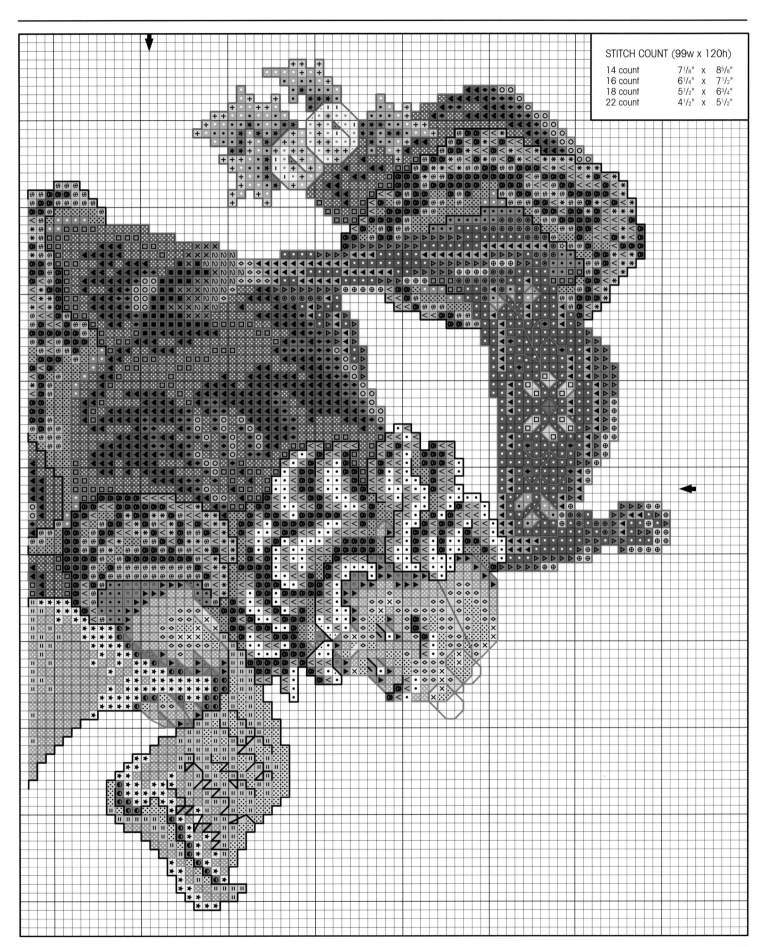

STITCH COUNT (99w x 120h)

count			
14 count	7¹⁄₈"	x	8⁵⁄₈"
16 count	6¹⁄₄"	x	7¹⁄₂"
18 count	5¹⁄₂"	x	6³⁄₄"
22 count	4¹⁄₂"	x	5¹⁄₂"

hooRAy foR chRistmas

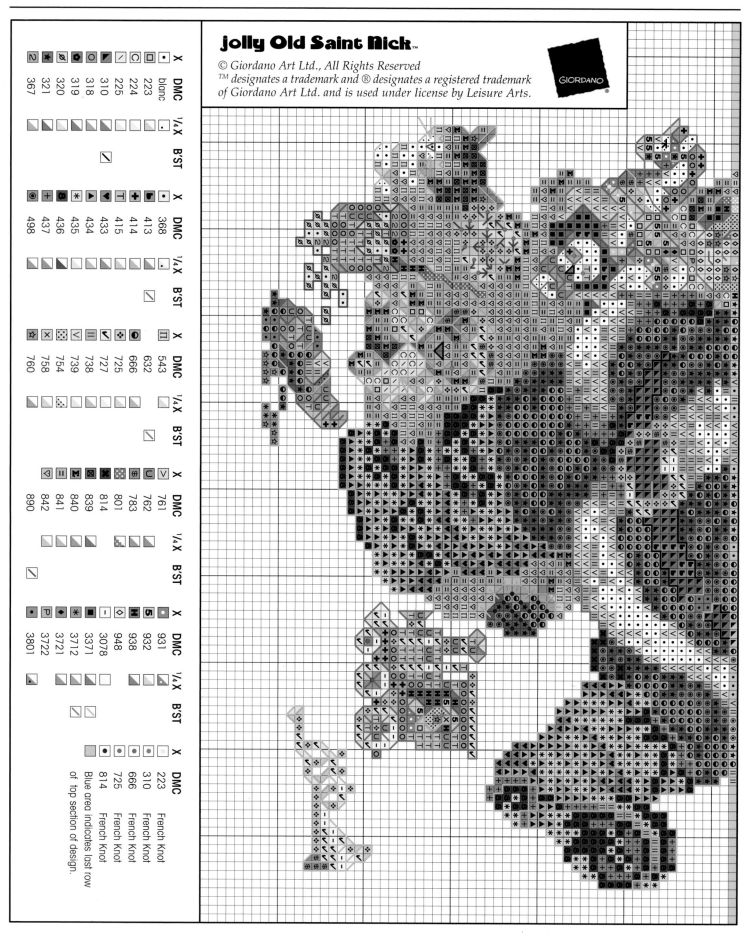

X									DMC
2	★	⊘	◆	⊘	◢	⟋	⟳	•	
367	321	320	319	318	310	225	224	223	blanc

¼X								

B'ST								
							⟍	

X									DMC
◉	＋	⊞	✶	▶	T	＋	⌐	•	
498	437	436	435	434	433	415	414	413	368

¼X								

B'ST								
				⟍				

X									DMC
☆	✕	⊡	⋁	＝	⬉	❖	◐	⊓	
760	758	754	739	738	727	725	666	632	543

¼X								

B'ST								
							⟍	

X									DMC
⬌	⊟	M	⊠	✚	⟐	＃	C	⋁	
890	842	841	840	839	814	801	783	762	761

¼X								

B'ST								
								⟍

X									DMC
•	P	◆	✳	▪	I	⊞	5	⊡	
3801	3722	3721	3712	3371	3078	948	938	932	931

¼X								
◣						◤		◥

B'ST								
			⟍				⟍	

X	DMC		
▨	223	French Knot	
●	310	French Knot	
●	666	French Knot	
●	725	French Knot	
□	814	French Knot	

Blue area indicates last row
of top section of design.

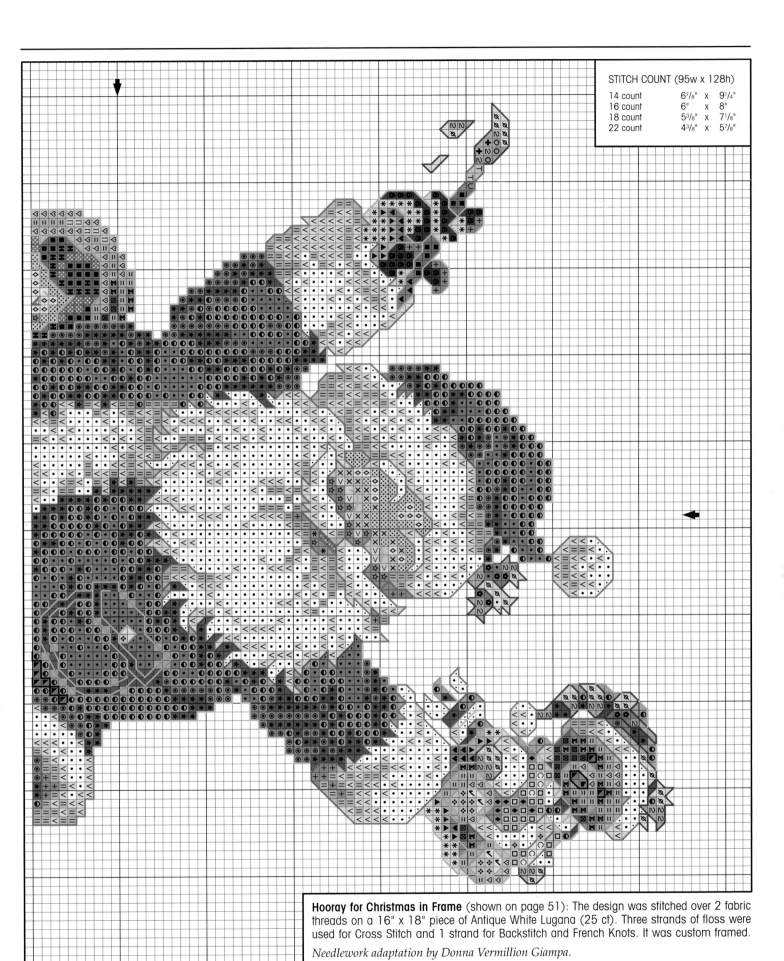

STITCH COUNT (95w x 128h)

14 count	6⅞"	x	9¼"
16 count	6"	x	8"
18 count	5⅜"	x	7⅛"
22 count	4⅜"	x	5⅞"

Hooray for Christmas in Frame (shown on page 51): The design was stitched over 2 fabric threads on a 16" x 18" piece of Antique White Lugana (25 ct). Three strands of floss were used for Cross Stitch and 1 strand for Backstitch and French Knots. It was custom framed.

Needlework adaptation by Donna Vermillion Giampa.

GENERAL INSTRUCTIONS

WORKING WITH CHARTS

How to Read Charts: Each of the designs is shown in chart form. Each colored square on the chart represents one Cross Stitch or one Half Cross Stitch. Each colored triangle on the chart represents one Quarter Stitch. In some charts, reduced symbols are used to indicate Quarter Stitches (**Fig. 1**). **Fig. 2** and **Fig. 3** indicate Cross Stitch under Backstitch.

Fig. 1   **Fig. 2**   **Fig. 3**

Black or colored dots on the chart represent Cross Stitch or French Knots. The black or colored straight lines on the chart indicate Backstitch. The symbol is omitted or reduced when a French Knot, Backstitch, or bead covers a square.

Each chart is accompanied by a color key. This key indicates the color of floss to use for each stitch on the chart. The headings on the color key are for Cross Stitch (**X**), DMC color number (**DMC**), Quarter Stitch (**¼X**), Half Cross Stitch (**½X**), and Backstitch (**B'ST**). Color key columns should be read vertically and horizontally to determine type of stitch and floss color. Some designs may include stitches worked with metallic thread, such as blending filament, braid, or cable. The metallic thread may be blended with floss or used alone. If any metallic thread is used in a design, the color key will contain the necessary information.

STITCHING TIPS

Working over Two Fabric Threads: Use the sewing method instead of the stab method when working over two fabric threads. To use the sewing method, keep your stitching hand on the right side of the fabric (instead of stabbing the fabric with the needle and taking your stitching hand to the back of the fabric to pick up the needle). With the sewing method, you take the needle down and up with one stroke instead of two. To add support to stitches, it is important that the first Cross Stitch be placed on the fabric with stitch 1-2 beginning and ending where a vertical fabric thread crosses over a horizontal fabric thread (**Fig. 4**). When the first stitch is in the correct position, the entire design will be placed properly, with vertical fabric threads supporting each stitch.

Fig. 4

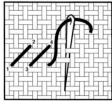

Attaching Beads: Refer to chart for bead placement and sew bead in place using a fine needle that will pass through bead. Bring needle up at 1, run needle through bead and then down at 2. Secure floss on back or move to next bead as shown in **Fig. 5**.

Fig. 5

STITCH DIAGRAMS

Note: Bring threaded needle up at 1 and all odd numbers and down at 2 and all even numbers.

Counted Cross Stitch (X): Work one Cross Stitch to correspond to each colored square on the chart. For horizontal rows, work stitches in two journeys (**Fig. 6**). For vertical rows, complete each stitch as shown (**Fig. 7**). When working over two fabric threads, work Cross Stitch as shown in **Fig. 8**. When the chart shows a Backstitch crossing a colored square (**Fig. 9**), a Cross Stitch should be worked first; then the Backstitch (**Fig. 14** or **15**) should be worked on top of the Cross Stitch.

Fig. 6   **Fig. 7**

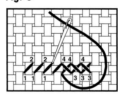

Fig. 8   **Fig. 9**

Quarter Stitch (¼X): Quarter Stitches are denoted by triangular shapes of color on the chart and on the color key. For a Quarter Stitch, come up at 1 (**Fig. 10**), then split fabric thread to go down at 2. **Fig. 11** shows the technique for Quarter Stitches when working over two fabric threads.

Fig. 10   **Fig. 11**

Half Cross Stitch (½X): This stitch is one journey of the Cross Stitch and is worked from lower left to upper right as shown in **Fig. 12**. When working over two fabric threads, work Half Cross Stitch as shown in **Fig. 13**.

Fig. 12   **Fig. 13**

Backstitch (B'ST): For outline detail, Backstitch (shown on chart and on color key by black or colored straight lines) should be worked after the design has been completed (**Fig. 14**). When working over two fabric threads, work Backstitch as shown in **Fig. 15**.

Fig. 14   **Fig. 15**

French Knot: Bring needle up at 1. Wrap floss once around needle and insert needle at 2, holding end of floss with non-stitching fingers (**Fig. 16**). Tighten knot, then pull needle through fabric, holding floss until it must be released. For larger knot, use more strands of floss; wrap only once.

Fig. 16

Instructions tested and photo items made by Arlene Allen, Lois Allen, Muriel Hicks, Pat Johnson, Patricia O'Neil, Angie Perryman, Anne Simpson, Lavonne Sims, Helen Stanton, and Trish Vines.